THE SECOND SPRING IN CHARNWOOD FOREST

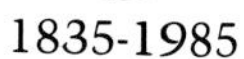

Published by
The East Midlands Studies Unit
of Loughborough University
in association with
Mount Saint Bernard Abbey
to celebrate the sesquicentenary
of their foundation.

John Henry Newman

THE SECOND SPRING IN CHARNWOOD FOREST

by Andrew C. Lacey

ERRATA

Page 15 "In 1835 he married and settled at Grace Dieu Hall . . ."

should read:- In 1833 he married, and settled at Grace Dieu Hall.

Page 17 "The Bishop (Dr Baines, O.S.B. Vicar Apostolic of the Western District) . . .

should read:- The Bishop (Rt Rev Dr Thomas Walsh, Vicar Apostolic of the Midland District) . . .

Page 21 "But by 1846 ten years after Odilo and his six monks . . ."

should read:- But by 1844 nine years after Odilo and his six monks . . .

Page 21 "in 1874 . . ."

should read:- In 1847 . . .

Page 31 "24th May 1836 . . ."

should read:- 24th May 1835 . . .

"Thrones are overturned, and are never restored; states live and die, and then are matters only for history. Babylon was great, and Tyre, and Egypt, and Nineveh, and shall never be great again. The English Church was, and the English Church was not, and the English Church is once again. This is the portent, worthy of a cry. It is the coming of a Second Spring; it is a restoration in the moral world, such as that which yearly takes place in the physical."

J.H. Newman

ISBN 0 946207 03 8

Phototypeset in Trump Mediaeval,
and designed and produced by
AB Printers Limited, Leicester, England

The front cover shows the Tower as seen from the gardens of Mount Saint Bernard Abbey, Charnwood Forest, Leicestershire

Table of Contents

Acknowledgements

I would like to thank Dr Marilyn Palmer without whom this work would never have seen the light of day, and Brother Jonathan Gell for providing me with so much help and material from the archives of Mount St Bernard.

Also Sr Mary Amelian and Sr Mary Magdalen of Our Lady's Convent, Loughborough for their help and the use of pictures from the Convent archives.

Plates are acknowledged as follows:

Mount St Bernard Abbey	—	1,2,3,4,6,7,9,10,11,15
Mr W. Wortley	—	16,17,18,19
Ratcliffe College	—	13,14
Our Lady's Convent, Loughborough	—	20
Leicestershire Record Office	—	12
National Portrait Gallery	—	5
National Gallery of Ireland	—	8

Abbreviations

I.C.	Institute of Charity (Rosminian)
M.S.B.	Mount St Bernard
O.C.S.O.	Order of Cistercians of Strict Observance (known as Trappists)
O.P.	Order of Preachers (Dominican)
O.S.B.	Order of St Benedict (Benedictines)

List of Plates

Chapter One

INTRODUCTION

The history of the Roman Catholic Revival in nineteenth century England can be approached from many angles — the history of Catholic education, the influence of the Romantic and Gothic revivals, the influence of Irish immigration, the importance of the Catholic gentry, the differences between English and Continental Catholicism, these are just a few. Whilst this contributes to the variety of the subject, it also makes it a very large one, particularly as it is well documented. This means that I have had to be very selective and confine myself to a relatively small area delineated by Loughborough, Grace Dieu Manor and Mount St Bernard, and even within this area I have only scratched the surface. Some of the points mentioned have not been developed as thoroughly as they might have been, particularly the interrelation of the depressed economy in the 1840s and the reactions to the Catholic missioners. Due to lack of space the establishment of Ratcliffe College has not been considered,[1] nor the reformatory at Mount St Bernard established by Abbot Burder in 1856,[2] neither has the development of the Dominican mission in Leicester been mentioned.[3] But what I have tried to do is show how the foundations of Catholicism were laid through the establishment of the Cistercian monastery and particularly the work of Gentili and the Rosminians. Even then the Rosminians have been treated on a strictly functional basis without a history of the Order. This is an unfortunate necessity because the Catholic Revival was a nationwide process with all the parts interacting to form an overall picture, and it is difficult to treat one small aspect of the Revival in isolation, and in the process important personalities, institutions and developments are excluded.

Another aim of this work is to demonstrate that the revival in the East Midlands was characterised by some important names and organisations. Augustus Welby Northmore Pugin, the famous Gothic revivalist, not only designed and built St Chad's, the Roman Catholic Cathedral in Birmingham and St Barnabas, Nottingham, but also on a more modest scale the Chapel of St Winefride's in Shepshed, the second monastery at Mount St Bernard and Ratcliffe College. He also submitted to Ambrose Phillipps (De Lisle) a plan, which was never executed, to rebuild Garendon Hall. John Talbot, Earl of Shrewsbury, was the leading Catholic aristocrat in the East Midlands as a whole, (Pugin also remodelled his home at Alton Towers) whilst Ambrose De Lisle fulfilled a similar role in Charnwood itself. De Lisle was instrumental in bringing Gentili to the area, and in settling the Cistercians in Charnwood Forest. So, what with Rosminian missions in Loughborough and Shepshed, the Missionary Oblates of Mary Immaculate at Grace Dieu, and the Dominican Order at Holy Cross Priory in Leicester, the Catholic Church was able to mobilise within a comparatively small area of wealth and influence, two major monastic orders, two teaching orders and also enlist the services of an architect of the calibre of Pugin.

This Catholic activity generated much opposition, and an important part of this work deals with the opposition of the Rev Francis Merewether at Whitwick, and two of the most famous controversies concerning Mount St Bernard during its foundation. It is often difficult in this perhaps post-Christian age to appreciate or understand the strength of feeling which was generated over religious questions. Yet if history is about understanding the past as well as documenting what happened, it is not good enough just to ignore those issues which are out of character with contemporary orthodoxy. Religion and religious controversies were very important in nineteenth century Britain, and the controversies over the Catholic Revival, linked as they were to the fear of anything considered foreign in any way, can be seen as a sort of magnet, drawing together arguments and opinions which were also employed in other controversies of the time. Chief among these was the belief that Papal allegiance made all Catholics, and particularly priests and members of religious orders, potential traitors; or the suspicion that missionary work was a front for all sorts of theocratic and political ambitions, which were aimed at subverting the Constitution and destroying the English way of life. This nationalistic criticism was echoed in the oft-quoted belief that Roman Catholicism might be suitable for Spanish peasants or South American Indians, but it was not fit for the English who would never submit to such an authoritarian superstition. This attitude was often accompanied by a whole string of traditional myths, such as the belief that Jesuits encouraged Catholics to assassinate Protestant rulers, or that the confessional was an instrument of immorality, or that Catholicism meant absolutist government, or that the Church deliberately brainwashed children in its doctrines; an alternative argument was that the Church deliberately kept people poor and stopped the spread of education, so as to keep its followers in superstitious ignorance. These myths were usually spiced with a few horror stories about imprisonment in convents or monasteries, or the activities of the Inquisition. The image of the Catholic priest therefore became a caricature of a shifty Machiavellian Jesuit, scheming and plotting ways to destroy the freedom of the people, the truths of Protestantism, and to replace them with the authority of Anti-Christ.

Such attitudes had been the stock-in-trade of English Protestantism for at least three centuries before Gentili and the Cistercians arrived in Charnwood Forest, and they remained the staple diet of Evangelicals, such as Merewether, and non-conformists until well into the twentieth century. Yet, particularly with Evangelical Anglicans, such as Merewether, the weakest point in their argument was the identification of the Anglican religious establishment with the social and economic establishment. This meant that if people became disillusioned or separated from one aspect of the establishment, whether through depression and poverty or through a significant social change, then their alienation would extend to other areas of the establishment. This is suggested as one of the reasons for the significant number of Catholic converts made during the 1840s, because in an age when the majority still believed religion to be very important Catholicism was an institution which was not connected with the traditional order of society. Most of the early converts were labourers, artisans or small shopkeepers, those who in 'normal' times could expect a reasonably secure if austere livelihood, but who in times of depression faced possible destitution; and the 1840s were a time of depression both in agriculture and the hosiery industry.

A time of depression and uncertainty

brings forth dissent from those affected. Yet it is an error to believe that all such dissent is necessarily radical; often such dissent is fundamentally negative rather than radical in that it reacts against a particular situation, without providing any alternative or possible changes. Thus in the 1840s some became Chartists or joined the agitation against the Poor Law, some went into the workhouse but many more, whilst taking no part in political agitation, became very disillusioned with the traditional order of society. The Established Church was felt to be indifferent to the effects of depression, preaching resignation and the maintenance of social distinction; whilst the aristocracy and gentry had largely abandoned any pretence of paternalism, in conformity to the dictates of Political Economy. Thus did many reject the twin pillars of Squire and Parson; the 'Protestant Settlement' had let them down.

Into this situation of disillusionment and alienation stepped a man such as Gentili, burning with missionary zeal, dedicated to helping the poor, setting up free day schools, marrying those who could not afford the licence fee and nearly being imprisoned for it, distributing alms, visiting people in their homes, preaching in the open air and, what is significant, presenting a simple but plausible reason for the depression and the distress. He claimed that it was all because of the Reformation; this had replaced Catholic charity with Protestant individualism. This was in marked contrast to what ordinary people had heard before, it was new, the missioners appeared to be genuinely concerned and Catholicism provided disorientated people with a sense of belonging and worth. It was by such tactics that the Primitive Methodists had also gained converts earlier in the century.

In a society still based upon religious foundations dissent from the establishment usually took the form of dissent from the establishment's religion, whether Anglican or non-conformist. That this dissent was not always radical is evidenced by the number of converts to Catholicism, as the Catholic Church was not a radical organisation; and there is no comparable influx of Catholics into the leadership of the early Trades Unions as there was with the Primitive Methodists. In that sense conversion to Catholicism could be termed negative dissent, and just as Methodism is often seen as the force which saved Britain from revolution in the early nineteenth century, so the revival of Catholicism, by providing a conservative outlet for those caught in the depression of the 1840s, contributed to the containing of what might have become a revolutionary situation.

Chapter Two

THE FOUNDATION OF MOUNT ST BERNARD

The Cistercian monastery of Mount St Bernard has its origins, as did so many Roman Catholic institutions established during the early part of the nineteenth century, in the French Revolution. The anti-clerical nature of the Revolution and the subsequent disruption and persecution forced many French Catholics, and particularly members of Religious Orders, to seek refuge in England. The origins of Mount St Bernard came through two lines which each stemmed from Lulworth in Dorset. Lulworth was the name of the estate of Mr Thomas Weld, head of a famous and ancient Catholic family, and it was here in 1794 that a group of Cistercian monks, originally from the Community of La Trappe, settled after they had missed the boat which was to have taken them to Canada. A future Abbot of Mount St Bernard, in fact the first English Abbot since the Reformation, Bernard Palmer, entered the Cistercian order at Lulworth in 1808.

In 1817, the Community at Lulworth took advantage of the restoration of the Bourbon Monarchy, and returned to Melleraie in France. The Community at Melleraie became a great centre of the Cistercian life, and of the one hundred and ninety five monks there during the 1820s, eighty were either English or Irish; Bernard Palmer, although not yet a priest, was Novice-Master, Guardian of the Rule and Sacristan to the Community. But the deposition of Charles X in 1830 meant that the Catholic Church, which had perhaps unwisely associated itself closely with the Bourbon regime, again came under fierce attack. The new government of King Louis Phillipe decided that all foreign Religious were to be expelled, and in November 1831 the English and Irish monks who refused to leave Melleraie were forcibly ejected by soldiers; in fact with four soldiers to one monk, one to a limb, they were literally carried out!

After this rather undignified exit, fifteen monks, including Bernard Palmer, retired to Nantes hoping to be able to re-enter Melleraie when times were quieter. Sixty four monks set sail for Cork, Ireland, where they joined Vincent Ryan, late Prior of Melleraie, who had gone to Ireland to search for a suitable site upon which the monks could establish a new community. In 1832 land was acquired in Co. Waterford upon which the new monastery was built and following the Cistercian tradition, was dedicated to Our Lady. As all Cistercian communities are dedicated to Our Lady they are usually designated by the name of the site upon which they are built so as to avoid confusion. Thus the new monastery became known as Mount Melleray and building was completed in 1838.

The second line from Lulworth which eventually contributed to the foundation of Mount St Bernard began in 1802 with the establishment of a Community of French Trappist Nuns, led by the indefatigable Madame de Chabannes, who had led her nuns to Russia and back in their attempts to escape from the forces of Revolution. Finally they were settled by Lord Arundel on land at Stapehill about fifteen miles from the Cistercian

Plate 1: Norbert Woolfrey

Plate 2: Ambrose de Lisle

monastery at Lulworth. In 1827 their Chaplain was one Odilo Woolfrey; he and his brother Norbert both came from an old Catholic family and had grown up virtually in the shadow of the Lulworth Community. They had both entered the Cistercian Order at Melleraie, Odilo being sent to Stapehill after his ordination. It would appear that neither Odilo nor Norbert were in France in 1831 to experience the unwelcome attention of the French soldiers, as Norbert appears to have joined his brother at Stapehill some months before the beginning of 1832. Whilst at Stapehill, Fr Norbert was approached by Vincent Ryan and asked to help raise money for the building of Mt Melleray; and it was during 1833, whilst Fr Norbert was acting as Deacon at a High Mass in St Mary's, Moorfield, London, that he first met Ambrose De Lisle and his fiancée Laura Clifford.

De Lisle (1809-78) who changed his name from Ambrose Lisle March Phillipps to Ambrose de Lisle in 1862 on succeeding his father as Squire of Garendon, was the eldest son of Charles March Phillipps of Garendon Hall and had been converted to Roman Catholicism in 1824 at the early age of fifteen. In 1835 he married and settled at Grace Dieu Hall, which is now used as a preparatory school for Ratcliffe College. It was De Lisle's burning ambition to further the spread of Catholicism by establishing a contemplative community in the Charnwood area, and to this end he invited Fr Norbert and Bishop Walsh, Vicar-Apostlic of the Midland district, to Grace Dieu during 1835 to discuss the venture.[1] The first move of Bishop Walsh was to contact Dom Antoine, the Abbot of Melleraie in France, which was then the Mother House of the Order in Britain and France. But Dom Antoine was of the opinion that he had little jurisdiction outside France, and that consequently the matter was in the hands of Bishop Walsh. So with a loan of £4,000 from the Bishop, De Lisle bought a property of over 200 acres from Mr Thomas Gisborne, MP, about two miles from Grace Dieu Hall. The loan was settled with the stipulation that interest was only to be paid when and if De Lisle succeeded his father as Squire of Garendon. This he did in 1862 and the loan and accumulated interest were paid off by 1899. The land they bought was known as Tin Meadow, and was largely barren apart from a small piece of cultivated land and a derelict four-roomed cottage. Odilo Woolfrey came to Grace Dieu from Stapehill at the request of Bishop Walsh, who informed him that he was to be Prior of the new foundation, whereupon he chose six English lay-brothers from Mt Melleray to join him as the nucleus of the new Community. Thus the two lines which had begun at Lulworth met at Mount St Bernard, when the monks from Mt Melleray joined Odilo and Norbert Woolfrey from Stapehill.

It is interesting to note the reactions which greeted the foundation of the Community. In a letter of November 1835, Odilo was emphasising that the Community was solely English. This is significant in view of the later success of Gentili and the Rosminians as it was felt that England would be more easily converted by English Catholics than by French or Italian missionaries sent specifically for that purpose. Lord Shrewsbury's reaction was that the whole venture was a mistake because the contemplative Cistercians would not be active in the spread of Catholicism. He suggested instead a Community of pastoral brothers particularly as:

> 'The new system of Poor Law makes it once more highly desirable to have almshouses where the poor forlorn wretches may find a comfortable asylum with the benefit of religion, instead of those horrid haunts the common workhouses.'[2]

However, in spite of Lord Shrewsbury's views the title deeds were exchanged on

29 September 1835 and a Brother was dispatched to take possession of the cottage, the only building on the site. When the rest of the Community followed shortly afterwards, there were seven living in this four-roomed house, living a life so spartan that in those early days the whole community survived on £1 a week. The cottage was in such a bad state of repair, that during the first winter, snow came through the roof and covered their beds! It was during this time that Bernard Palmer left Nantes, where he had been living since 1831, and settled at Mount St Bernard. The following letter written by Palmer to Madame de Chabannes at Stapehill during November 1836 is worth quoting at some length as it gives a vivid impression of life at Tin Meadow during the early years where he talks about the building of the first monastery and the problems that it was causing:

'Things go on here as well as can be expected... our dormitory is finished and the Refectory and we have just begun the Chapel. Money is the chief thing that is wanting here, everything is going out and very little coming in, for Fr Norbert has left off begging for us these three or four months, and Br Luck (Luke Levermore) has gathered but little lately, who is now returned from London, so I leave you to judge of our present circumstances... Mr Phillipps (De Lisle) has bought the land for us and helps us all he can, but as his father allows him but a very small income he cannot do much. If we rub on until next harvest we shall not have our wheat to buy as we have sown about eight acres of wheat. Our land is very good when one's tilled, but it is expensive to till on account of the quantity of very large stones...

By the desire of the Bishop, Fr Odilo and by express order of the Revd Fr Vincent Ryan, I am obliged to go visit the sick and the new converts and to catechise the latter, which takes me in general two days and a half in the week, for I have to go to three different parishes; now you know it is quite contrary to out state, but there is two or three observations to be made. First, it is only on those conditions that our land is given to us, and that our Bishop protects us. Secondly there is no priest in the neighbourhood. Rev'd Fr Vincent remarked when he was here that our holy Fr St Benedict went out of his cell to encourage the faithful in the time of persecution, therefore, to refuse the poor people instructions that desire it, and ask, it would be cruel to refuse them...

We have many converts, two of them died a few days ago after having received the Sacraments in the best disposition and with every marks of being the elect of God. One of them is a young man of twenty one years of age who had been converted about of three months, who had been three times to Confession and twice Communion, and the new converts walked in procession after the corpse with little white crosses on their breasts hanging about their necks with white ribbons. It was very consoling to see the cross triumphing in a place where two years ago they hardly heard speak of a cross.[3]

Palmer's complaint about undertaking mission work and the incompatibility with the contemplative life, was part of a wider problem which faced the Catholic Church in England at that time, namely the dependence hitherto on the Catholic gentry. In a letter from De Lisle to Bishop Walsh dated April 22nd 1836 De Lisle stipulated:

'That the monastery shall supply the Grace Dieu Mission with a daily Mass and all other ecclesiastical duties for ever, unless the Possessor of Grace Dieu and Garendon in conjunction with that of the Diocese shall otherwise appoint.'[4]

Such a request was totally at variance with the Cistercian tradition, but was part of the legacy of the fact that since the Reformation, Roman Catholicism in England had survived principally in the private chapels of the Catholic nobility and gentry. This was true, for example, of the Catholic mission in Leicester, which was established in 1746 by John Beaumont-Byerley in his house at Belgrave, his private chapel serving as a Mass centre. The priest, Fr John Clarkson OP was a blend of mission priest (in which capacity he would enter Leicester disguised as a labourer, as these were still penal days) and a private chaplain to Beaumont-Byerley. Priests in such circumstances were usually totally dependent on their patrons who came to exercise more practical control over Catholic activities in England than the Bishops appointed Vicars-Apostolic. Thus, amongst other things, the Emancipation Act ended the reliance on the Catholic gentry for sanctuary and protection which had long been a feature of English Catholicism.

Unfortunately not all the Catholic gentry appreciated the change, and De Lisle at this point appears to have had visions of himself as being the patron of a Mass-centre from which priests would issue under his authority to convert Leicestershire, Grace Dieu being the hub of Catholicism in the area. It was to be over this very issue that De Lisle and Gentili clashed later. By 1839, when the Founder's Deed was signed, De Lisle had been persuaded to abandon the idea of Mount St Bernard furnishing Grace Dieu chapel with priests because: 'the duties of the Mission are incompatible with the Cistercian Order.'[5]

The post-Emancipation Church was determined to avoid, so far as was practical, being dependent on the Catholic gentry. So under the terms of the Founder's Deed, signed on the Feast of St Michael 1839, it was agreed that the area of land comprising Tin Meadow was to be granted to the Cistercian order in perpetuity without rent, charge or other encumbrances. In return, weekly Masses for De Lisle and his wife, were to be celebrated at the monastery, a request which is still honoured, and one High and thirty Low Requiem Masses on the death of the head of the family or his wife.

Meanwhile, in the short space of two years, the monks in the cottage at Tin Meadow had built themselves a temporary monastery in the 'Elizabethan' style, the same one which was causing Bernard Palmer such financial worries. It was designed and built by William Railton, who had previously designed Grace Dieu Hall and was later to be responsible for Nelson's Column in Trafalgar Square.[6] As Palmer mentions in his letter to Madame de Chabannes, by November 1836 the chapel was under construction and the dormitory and refectory completed. The chapel was dedicated on 11 October 1837; and a report appeared in the *Staffordshire Examiner* which vividly conveys the almost medieval splendour which was to be seen in Charnwood only eight years after the Emancipation Act:

> 'at an early hour, the Bishop with his clergy accompanied by Sir Charles Wolseley Bt in court dress, and Mr Ambrose Phillipps, who wore his uniform as Deputy-Lieutenant of the County, walked up by a beautiful private road from Grace Dieu to the entrance of the monastery land, a distance of about two miles.'

The procession was headed by a crucifer in cassock and surplice, followed by six acolytes similarly robed and many banners. The Bishop (Dr Baines, OSB Vicar-Apostolic of the Western District) was:

> 'vested in full pontificals, with his mitre and crozier, and his train borne by an acolyte in a white surplice. The choir monks were dressed in white habits and

cowls and the lay Brothers in brown habits, according to the rule of the Cistercian order.'[7]

The Hon Rev George Spencer, youngest son of the second Earl Spencer (of Althorp Hall) who had 'gone over to Rome' in 1830: 'pronounced a most eloquent eulogium on the nature of the monastic state.' After the Pontifical High Mass the ladies were given lunch in the Guest House, the men:

'partook of a monastic repast consisting of eggs and fruit in the refectory of the monks, at the same time the monks took their own dinner during which one of the brotherhood, according to custom, read a spiritual letter.'

After that Vespers were:

'solemnly chanted, and an admirable sermon was preached by the Very Rev Dr Wendell the President of Oscott College.'[8]

With the temporary monastery finished, and well and truly dedicated, the first postulants were accepted and Vincent Ryan sent more Brothers over from Mt Melleray. Thus within ten years of Emancipation a thriving and permanant Cistercian Community was established in the heart of England, almost exactly three hundred years after the dissolution of the medieval Cistercian Monastery at Garendon by Henry VIII.[9]

Plate 3: The Monastery designed by William Railton

Plate 4: The Refectory in Railton's Monastery

Chapter Three

PUGIN, SHREWSBURY AND PALMER

Mount St Bernard was a Priory until 1848, and a Prior rather than an Abbot is the head of a community which does not have Abbey status, and the Prior's assistant is known as a Sub-Prior. When Mount St Bernard was raised to Abbey status, the Prior's title was changed to that of Abbot and his assistant became known as Prior rather than Sub-Prior. Odilo Woolfrey remained as Prior until late 1839 when Benedict Johnson was appointed in his place. Johnson remained in the post just over a year, being succeeded by Bernard Palmer in 1841. Both Woolfrey and Johnson acted as Sub-Priors for Palmer, Woolfrey until 1846 when both he and his brother Norbert departed for Australia with the intention of founding a Cistercian Community there; however this proved to be impossible and both brothers spent the remainder of their lives as Mission Priests, building up the Catholic community in the new colony. Odilo died in 1856 at Sydney and Norbert in 1872 at Waveley. Johnson served as sub-prior after Woolfrey's departure in 1846 and became Prior when Palmer was raised to the rank of Abbot in 1848.

John Talbot, Earl of Shrewsbury, was, as has been mentioned, the head of the principal Catholic family in the Midlands, and spared no effort, after Emancipation, to further the spread of Catholicism. In spite of his earlier reservations about the amount of money De Lisle spent on establishing a contemplative community, after visiting the monks in their first monastery he was so impressed that he decided to further their work by providing them with larger premises. Consequently he provided £2,000 towards the project and commissioned A.W.N. Pugin, whom he had recently employed to embellish his home at Alton Towers, to design a new monastery. Pugin, who leapt at the opportunity of designing a Gothic setting for a contemplative community, provided his services free of charge. Amongst his many talents was the ability to execute brilliant designs on a very limited budget, thus he built the Chapel of St Winefride's in Shepshed for £700. He saved money at Mount St Bernard by demanding no commission, by only using local stone, principally granite from Charnwood Forest and enlisting the monks into the work of dressing and hauling the stone. Thus the cost was kept to a minimum. As has been mentioned the initial cost was met of the Earl of Shrewsbury, but the monks themselves helped towards meeting the expenses. Palmer records that in 1842-3 fund raising events were held in Liverpool, Preston and Manchester, all of them areas with a significant Catholic population whether indigenous or Irish. The original section of the present monastery was opened in 1844 (it is being expanded all the time to meet changing needs, amongst other alterations the Chapter House was built by Pugin's son and opened in 1860, a clock tower was added, the nave transepts and Bell Tower of the Abbey Church were built in the 1930s and within the last ten years the Guest-House has been significantly enlarged. Fortunately all these additions have been designed so as to blend with

Plate 5: Augustus Welby Northmore Pugin, 1802-1852

Pugin's original, so that the present monastery gives the impression of an organic whole and not a jumble of conflicting styles). The choir of the Abbey Church was not completed until about two years after the monastery buildings, which caused some problems in that the monks did not wish to leave Railton's monastery until the new church was finished. But by 1846, ten years after Odilo and his six monks had moved into the broken down cottage at Tin Meadow, thirty monks and novices moved into a permanent, specifically designed building, built by one of the most famous and accomplished architects of the day. Pugin himself said of his work that:

> 'The whole of the buildings are erected in the greatest severity of the lancet style, with massive walls and buttresses, long and narrow windows, high gables and roofs with deeply arched doorways. Solemnity and simplicity are the characteristics of the monastery and every portion of the architecture and fittings corresponds to the authority of the Order for whom it has been raised.'

The culmination of this first major building project at Mount St Bernard came in 1874 when, to complement Gentili's Calvary at Grace Dieu erected four years earlier, the Calvary at Mount St Bernard was established on its present site overlooking the choir of the Abbey and providing a focal point for the public gardens.

The new monastery attracted many visitors, such as William Wordsworth, Florence Nightingale and Mr Gladstone as well as many well known continental Catholics such as Dollinger the great German theologian, Mondalembert and Lacondaire the French liberal Catholics, even the Comte de Chambord the Bourbon pretender to the throne of France. Mount St Bernard also attracted the attention of the English Catholic community, Ullathorne who became the first Bishop of Birmingham in 1850 was a frequent visitor, as was Nicholas Wiseman who was Coadjutor of the Central District between 1840 and 1847 before his installation as the first Cardinal Archbishop of Westminster. The archives at Mount St Bernard record Wiseman paying four visits to the monastery in 1841-2 and again in 1844 when he preached at the consecration of Pugin's Abbey Church.

Another early visitor who was to become famous in later life was Henry Manning, who as Cardinal Manning was to succeed Wiseman as Archbishop of Westminster in 1865. Manning, who until 1851 was an Anglican archdeacon at Oxford, was deeply influenced by the Oxford Movement and, like many other Tractarians, he visited Mount St Bernard in April 1850 whilst staying with De Lisle at Grace Dieu Manor. This visit occurred one month after the famous 'Gorham Judgement' in which the Judicial Committee of the Privy Council, at that time the final arbiter in Anglican Church affairs, had overruled the Bishop of Exeter's refusal to appoint the Rev G.C. Gorham to the living of Bampton Speke in Devon, because of his unsound views on Baptismal Regeneration. This intervention by a secular body in the discipline of the Church convinced many High Churchmen, Manning amongst them, that the Church of England was not in a position to maintain or teach Catholic doctrine whilst still tied to the State; and a year later Manning was received into the Catholic Church.

His second visit to Mount St Bernard was in June 1851, two months after his conversion, and twelve days before his ordination as a Catholic priest. Thus his visits to De Lisle and Mount St Bernard were probably part of the process of his conversion. That he found the visits invigorating physically as well as spiritually is apparent from a letter to George Ryder, his relation through marriage, when he mentions that: 'I often

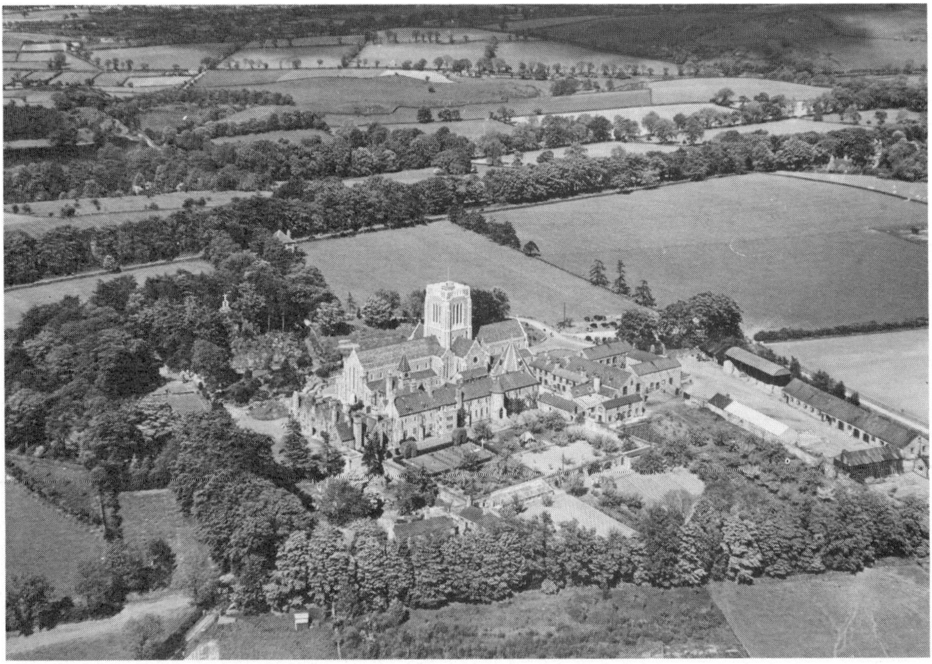

Plate 6: Mount St. Bernard Abbey
Plate 7: The Guest House of the Abbey

think of the wild walks over Charnwood Forest.'[1]

But perhaps the most famous of the Oxford Reformers, and certainly one of the most influential 'personalities', if not one of the greatest minds of the nineteenth century, to be connected with Mount St Bernard was John Henry Newman. He had been brought up as an Evangelical Anglican, but at Oxford he was deeply influenced by the High Churchmanship of Richard Hurrell Froude, later to be one of the instigators of the Oxford Movement. Newman became a fellow of Oriel College in 1822, and from 1828 to 1843 he was vicar of St Mary's Oxford. In 1833 Newman wrote the first of what were to become the famous 'Tracts for the Times' (hence the title Tractarians) which attempted to interpret Anglicanism in terms of Catholic doctrine, and demonstrate that the Church of England was in direct apostolic descent from the Ancient Church of the first thousand years and that its doctrine contained nothing contrary to pre-Tridentine Catholicism. Of the ninety tracts which were produced between 1833 and 1841 Newman wrote twenty-six, including Tract 90 wherein Newman argued that the Thirty-Nine Articles, the doctrinal 'constitution' of the Church of England, were not essentially different from Roman Catholic teaching. This caused a great controversy; Newman was accused of being a crypto-papist and no more tracts were produced.

Newman increasingly withdrew from University life and controversy after the publication of Tract 90 to the Chapel at Littlemore, just outside Oxford. Here, with a few friends, he lived a strict regular life and studied the Fathers of the early Church. With hindsight it is possible to see that the logical outcome of this life was his conversion to Rome. He himself admitted as such a year before he resigned from St Mary's, when in a letter he confessed rather light-heartedly, that:

> 'I am an incipient monk, in my novitiate at least. I am preparing a monastery at Littlemore, and shall shortly retire from the world — so that if the great prospects are destined for me you speak of, I shall be the first bishop from the Cloister for the last three hundred years — and while I am about it, I think, I will not come out of it except for the Papacy.'[2]

In 1845 Newman did come out of his Cloister for the Papacy and was received into the Church by Dominic Barberi of the Passionists. Newman immediately embarked on a tour of the main centres of Catholicism in England and on the 6 January 1846 arrived at Ratcliffe College which he described as 'a very handsome building'. He then moved to Charnwood and whilst staying with De Lisle at Grace Dieu, lunched with the Rosminians in Loughborough and visited Mount St Bernard for the first time. Although this was his first visit, he had been corresponding with Bernard Palmer for about two years, for in 1844, a year before Newman was received into the Church, Palmer mentions his correspondence with Newman in a letter to Lord Shrewsbury. Unfortunately the correspondence between Palmer and Newman has not survived. In a letter to a friend, Newman commented that:

> 'I was three nights at Mr Phillipps and went to see the Trappists who are wonderful.'[3]

On completion of his tour of Catholic England, Newman went to Rome where he entered the College of Propaganda and joined the Oratorians. It was as an Oratorian living at the house he had opened at Maryvale, Birmingham, the previous February that Newman paid his second visit to Mount St Bernard, from 25 July to 3rd August 1848, on retreat. Newman's diary records that he was asked to speak to the Community in Chapter and talked with Bernard Palmer whilst they walked about the farm as well

Plate 8: Cardinal Nicholas Wiseman

as dining with De Lisle at Garendon. It is apparent from his diary entries that Mount St Bernard exercised a great influence on Newman, he wrote in mock despair on his arrival that:

'They are going to make me assist at the huge Antiphonals all through the Office through the week — I suspect I shall not escape *one* day's attendance — how shall I support it?'[4]

Newman was engaged at that time in planning the future of the Oratorians in England, and he took the opportunity of the peace and seclusion at Mount St Bernard to draw up his draft of the future strategy for the Oratory in England. As well as this it was agreed during his retreat that the Monks of Mount St Bernard would pray for the Oratorians on the feast of St Philip Neri, their founder, whilst on the feast of St Bernard of Clairvaux the Birmingham Oratorians would pray for the Community at Mount St Bernard. The practice is continued today.

Although this is the last recorded visit Newman made to Mount St Bernard the memory of his stay remained with him, for De Lisle records that in his correspondence with him Newman often mentioned the 'holy monks', and enquired after their welfare. But quite apart from the visits of the rich and famous were the tourists who came to Mount St Bernard in their hundreds. Palmer, it would appear, had had experience of visitors before, as he had begun his monastic life at Lulworth as Guestmaster and had often had to deal with visitors who were bitterly opposed to Catholicism and had come with the sole intention of discovering things with which to attack the Community. Now he had to deal not with opponents but with numbers and, as is demonstrated by the following letter he wrote to the *Leicester Chronicle,* that could be an even bigger problem:

'Sir, May I be allowed the privilege, through the medium of your valuable journal, of informing the public that owing to the daily increasing concourse of visitors to our humble solitude and the great annoyance arising therefrom, and specially by some reason of impropriety of conduct of *some* of the many: I am reluctantly forced to shut the gates of the monastery henceforth to all such visitors as may be called 'parties of pleasure', who come with the intention of making their refections on the rocks and other places of the premises. Hitherto we have exercised every possible condescension in this respect for the satisfaction of all parties, but we find this our condescension is much abused and hence we are necessitated to check the abuse.'[5]

Palmer was born in 1782 of Anglican parents at Charmouth in Dorset, and was in his early life an enthusiastic member of the Church of England, as is evidenced by the following extract from a letter he wrote to a Dr Oliver of Exeter: 'Judge of my devotion to the Church of England, when I tell you that I burnt the Pope in effigy, three or four years successively with great zeal.'[6]

The reaction of Dr Oliver is not recorded, but as Palmer was received into the Catholic Church at the age of twenty four, he probably ascribed it to youthful zeal. It was, perhaps, an indication that Palmer had an intense nature and that once he gave his allegiance he remained deeply committed. There is also the fact that very soon after burning the Pope in effigy he became a Roman Catholic, which suggests that such extreme behaviour might have been an attempt to smother doubts. J.H. Newman had also demonstrated early, but more sophisticated, zeal for the Church of England before becoming a Roman Catholic in 1845. Perhaps the characters of Newman and Palmer were similar in that both were unconsciously seeking a home. Both had shown early

Plate 9: The Abbey Church from the East

Plate 10: The West Cloister, Mount St Bernard Abbey

devotion to Anglicanism before renouncing it, and both found their peace in the all embracing security of Tridentine Catholicism.

Whilst living in London he attended Catholic services and was impressed by what he saw, so he went to Fr Wild at Warwick Street Chapel for instruction, before obtaining a post in service at Lulworth Castle through the Catholic publisher, Booker. He was received into the Church in 1806 at Lulworth and entered the monastery there two years later. Palmer's moves to France and back to Mount St Bernard in 1836 have been documented elsewhere, but since entering Lulworth he had taught himself to read and write and had studied successfully for his ordination which took place, probably at Oscott College, in 1838. He was wherever he went a popular figure, and appears to have been an uncomplicated, generous man who believed in his religion and his Cistercian vocation and tried to live both in depth. In January 1841 came his election as Prior, succeeding Woolfrey and Johnson, and during the following two years Palmer was busy overseeing the construction of Pugin's monastery; he appears to have taken a particular interest in the fund-raising activities taking place in Lancashire at that time.

One of the traditional functions of monasteries was to give alms to the poor, although how far this was actually practised in the Middle Ages and how far it is part of a later romantic idea is difficult to say, but the relief of poverty was practised at Mount St Bernard almost from its inception. *The Catholic Magazine* for October 1838 says of Mount St Bernard: 'The poor almost continuously surround the habitation of the monks to receive their daily allowance.' And ten years later Edmond Lafond on a visit to Mount St Bernard recorded the following sight:

> 'A crowd of poor people are fed and given lodging each day at the monastery ...I arrived in front of a great arched doorway which forms a gothic porch, where a crowd of beggars were sitting on stone benches.'[7]

The Census returns for 1851 reveal that six Irish paupers were then living in the Monastery, four of them were over fifty, which in terms of 1851 made them old men. For many the monastery was preferable to the workhouse when they were too old to earn a living.

Palmer was very concerned that the monastery should help the poor as much as possible. In 1846 he wrote to Lady Shrewsbury that:

> 'We have at present four little orphan children (Irish) whom I am having instructed. Last night one or two and twenty slept here without a home and in the greatest distress.'[8]

But it is in a letter Palmer wrote to *The Tablet* in March 1851 that the real extent of the monastery's almsgiving is realised, as he quotes the following figures of those relieved:

	Food	*Lodging*
1847	*36,374*	*12,144*
1848	*32,521*	*6,753*
1849	*30,020*	*5,939*
1850	*29,354*	*4,927*
	128,269	*29,763*

Of these numbers four-fifths were Irish, and it is significant that so many Irish should have turned for relief to the Church whereas the English poor did not do so to the same extent. There is also a noticeable drop in the numbers coming for relief between 1847 and 1850, perhaps due to the recovery of trade and agriculture which ended the 'hungry forties', and which would have reduced the number of the destitute. But, as Palmer says: 'this charity to body and soul could not be accomplished without great labour and expense.[9]

In 1848 three important briefs arrived from Rome. The first raised the Com

Plate 11: Bernard Palmer, 1794-1852, first Abbot of Mount St. Bernard

munity to Abbey status, and declared it to be the Mother House of the Cistercian Order in England. Following on from this, the second brief united Mount St Bernard to the General Chapter of the Cistercian Congregation of Strict Observance in France. The third brief confirmed the election of Palmer as Abbot which had taken place the previous November, and in the February 1849 he was blessed by Ullathorne who, during the following two years would be installed as the first Bishop of Birmingham. Palmer thus became the first Abbot of an English monastery to be created since the Reformation, but his heart had never been strong and with the onset of dropsy, he died on November 10 1852. He had been associated with the restoration of the Cistercian life in England since the beginning of Lulworth and he saw Mount St Bernard fully established as a thriving centre of the contemplative life. His death was mourned by many who had known him, and marked the depth of his devotion and the extent of his work for his Order and the spread of Catholicism. *The Tablet* recorded that:

> 'It may be said with truth that with difficulty could there be found even one person in the whole neighbourhood who had not received some signal benefit at the hands of Fr Bernard.[10]

That the regard in which he was held extended beyond the Catholic world is demonstrated by the following letter from an Anglican clergyman:

> 'I deeply sympathise with your venerable house on the loss of your truly pious and single-minded brother and Abbot. He impressed everyone of every class, who had the happiness to see and hear him, with the beauty of holiness. He was, indeed, a heavenly-minded man.'[11]

1852 also witnessed the deaths of John Talbot, Earl of Shrewsbury, and Pugin, and with regard to the Catholic revival, it marked the end of the foundation period. The Community at Mount St Bernard was settled and expanding; through the work of Gentili and other missioners the parish structure had been laid down in the area, and a significant number of converts gained. Ratcliffe College and Loughborough Convent were set on a firm foundation and the Episcopal Hierarchy had been restored two years previously. Thus within twenty-five years of Emancipation, the Catholic Church in Charnwood was restored fully to life, largely through the efforts of characters such as Palmer, Gentili and the Woolfreys, backed by De Lisle, Shrewsbury, Pugin and others who worked so hard to lay the foundations upon which others would build.

Plate 12: Rev. Francis Merewether, Vicar of Whitwick and Coleorton

Chapter Four

OPPOSITION — MEREWETHER, ANNE FULLARD AND THE JEFFREYS' CASE

Ever since the Reformation, and certainly since the reign of 'Bloody Mary', Roman Catholicism had been looked upon with suspicion and in many cases downright hatred. For generations raised on *Foxe's Book of Martyrs* and horror stories concerning the Spanish Inquisition *auto-da-fes* and other lurid tales of Catholic atrocities, Roman Catholicism evoked images of a dominant clergy, lording it over a cowering populace who were kept deliberately ignorant so as not to challenge the position of the Church, and that underneath every Church and Monastery were torture chambers ready to receive those who would not bend the knee. Catholics were also considered to be potential traitors in that they gave allegiance to a foreign power, namely the Papacy, and were thus to be excluded from public life and regarded with suspicion mingled with fear.[1] If twentieth century Americans would rather be dead than red, so many English for centuries after the Reformation would rather have been dead than Roman.

Given the strength of these attitudes, it is hardly surprising that the advent of a Cistercian Monastery in Charnwood Forest should have caused a few raised eyebrows amongst the Protestants of the neighbouring area, and in particular amongst the evangelical section of the community. One such individual, who over the next fifteen years did a lot of eyebrow raising over Mount St Bernard, was the Rev Francis Merewether, MA. He had been presented to the living of Coleorton in 1810 by Sir George Beaumont, Bt, of Coleorton Hall and in 1819 Merewether became Vicar of Whitwick as well. He remained Vicar of both livings for nearly fifty years, dying in 1864.

He was a prolific writer of decidedly 'Low Church' views and his first sortie against Mount St Bernard appeared on 24 May 1836 when he preached a sermon in Whitwick Parish Church entitled 'Popery, A New Religon, Compared With That of Christ and His Apostles.' When it is considered that the title deeds to Tin Meadow were not exchanged until 29 September, it is clear that it was known four or five months previously that plans existed for the founding of a monastic community.

In his sermon, Merewether contrasted the 'newness' of 'Popery' with Apostolic Christianity and denounced transubstantiation, Mariology, the communion of saints, purgatory and prayers for the dead, all of which, he claims, were added later. Then he announced that:

> 'the time is approaching, or rather is already come, when you will be within far too easy reach of being told that the religion of Christ and the religion of the Pope are of the same date.'[2]

A warning of what was seen as one of the dangers arising from the proximity of the new Cistercian Community. The proceeds from the sale of copies of this sermon (it was printed by W. Hextall of Ashby and sold by various people in London and by one D. Cartwright of Loughborough) were to go towards a proposed 'Whitwick Scriptural Society for the Maintenance of Apostolic Truth' which was intended to be the main focus of opposition to the spread of Catholicism in the Whitwick-Coalville area. Unfortunately for Merewether it never got off the ground.

In December 1835, Odilo Woolfrey published an account which was to create a great controversy, and was to provide Merewether with much new ammunition with which to attack Mount St Bernard and Catholicism in general; the controversy became known as the Anne Fullard case. She was an epileptic from Whitwick, who had a great desire to become a Catholic. Because of this she would attend the services in the Chapel at Grace Dieu, where, one evening, she had an epileptic attack. She was taken from the Chapel into the Hall where the attack got worse; according to Odilo's account she was becoming increasingly violent and was not responding to any treatment which they could give her. In the end, a medal was produced which, it was claimed, was miraculous, and Odilo placed this near her heart, whereupon she recovered. The history of the 'Miraculous Medals', for there were more than one, is that in 1830, a 'Sister of Charity' in Paris had a vision of the Virgin Mary who foretold the revolution against Charles X and the subsequent attack upon the Church. She commanded that medals be struck with Her image upon them. The nun obeyed and they were blessed by the Archbishop of Paris,

> 'and ever since that time they have wrought innumerable miracles in France, England and other countries.'[3]

Here was precisely the sort of thing Merewether had been warning his parishioners against, and in March 1836 he published his reply to Odilo's account of the cure. It was entitled 'Special Pleadings in the Court of Reason and Conscience. Held on Sunday March 20 1836. Trial of W.O. Woolfrey, and others, for Conspiracy', and it took the form of a dialogue between Woolfrey as defendant and a prosecuting counsel (but as prosecution, jury and judge were one and the same person, namely Merewether, the 'verdict' was a forgone conclusion!) This reply, he claimed, was written out of an:

> 'anxious desire to undeceive the poor and simple folk, whom you (Woolfrey) and your associates are endeavouring to pervert to the ruin of their souls.'[4]

Plate 13: Grace Dieu Hall

The 'verdict' of reason was that Woolfrey had failed in the discrediting of a Protestant Minister (Merewether), although in Woolfrey's account of the cure Merewether is never mentioned. He had failed to produce adequate proof of the facts concerning the case, and had failed to inspire beliefs in a miraculous cure. Woolfrey was then urged to stop teaching that salvation was to be achieved:

> 'on the merit of their own doings, on the prayers of saints, on the intercession of the Virgin, whom thou has exalted from the rank of being blessed among women, to be Queen of Heaven, lest, I say, all your superstitious and idolatrous worship should be laid to thy charge, and falling on thy head should overwhelm thee with a far more exceeding and eternal weight of misery, and drown thee in the depths of perdition.'[5]

Conscience upheld 'brother reason' and urged Woolfrey to repent. Also during the 'trial' great play was made of the fact that the medal was placed on the woman's breast so as to be near her heart. There followed a lengthy discussion of the differences between breast and bosom, and reference was made to the celibate life lived by Catholic Religious and Priests. All this was, of course, designed to blacken the name of monks and to play upon fears of lecherous priests living 'unnatural' celibate lives.

By April 1836 another tract had appeared entitled 'The Grace Dieu Miracle' which attacked De Lisle who had witnessed the cure and had signed Woolfrey's account of the proceedings, produced in the previous December. In a letter to Bishop Walsh of 22nd April De Lisle enclosed a copy of this pamphlet and expressed his regret at 'all the noise which Anne Fullard's cure has made in the Tory newspapers'.

But he believed that it would soon blow over.

> 'in this opinion Mr Lythgoe, the Jesuit, entirely concurs, he wrote me a letter about it in which he quite laughed at the Tories and said it would be a three day wonder and would then be forgotten.'[6]

Plate 14: Grace Dieu Chapel

Thus, right from its inception, indeed, almost before its inception, the Community at Mount St Bernard was a centre of controversy.

We now move to 1845 and the opening of the monastery designed by A.W.N. Pugin, and the Rev Francis Merewether is again ready to denounce the existence of the monastery in 'A Pastoral Address to the inhabitants of Whitwick, Leicestershire on the Opening of a Monastery within the limits of that Parish. With a Supplement'. This was also printed and sold by W. & J. Hextall of Ashby-de-la-Zouch. The address is worth looking at in some detail, because it contains most of the arguments used against the spread of Catholicism.

Merewether visited the Monastery whilst it was under construction in June 1844 and the address is another general attack on 'Popery' along the lines of the 'Popery a New Religion' sermon of 1835, only this time there is more detailed consideration of the monastic state, and particularly Mount of St Bernard, which he claimed was the first to be opened since: 'they were by the wisdom of the English State and Nation suppressed and abolished'.[7] In fact Railton's Monastery, dedicated in 1837, was the first purely English foundation since the Reformation. He declared, quite rightly, although much to his annoyance, that the prime purpose of the monastery was to strengthen Catholicism in England as a whole, and the Midlands area in particular. His general attitude to monasticism was that it had had its advantages in its time, and he mentions some of these advantages, namely the fostering of learning, quietness and 'Holy contemplation'[8] hospitality and the religious instruction of the young. But he did not believe that monasticism had any relevance for the nineteenth century.[9] To set against those advantages, Merewether also stressed the disadvantages; chief among these was that monasteries 'encouraged begging under the pretext of religion'.[10] They also sheltered lazy monks, and 'encouraged wicked practices...too gross in their nature to be here specifically described.[11] (He then provides footnotes, referring the interested reader to works wherein these 'wicked practices' are expanded upon). He also emphasised the fact that the Emancipation Act demanded that all Religious should register with a local JP and that it forbade immigration of Religious under the pain of perpetual banishment.[12]

At this point he moves on to a critique of Catholicism in general and Mount St Bernard in particular, by first denouncing the infallibity of the Church, which was Church doctrine until 1870, when Pius IX defined the doctrine of Papal infallibity; the universalist claims of the Papacy, transubstantiation, purgatory and priestly absolution. (He also refers to the nature of the Mass, Images, the Communion of Saints and regrets that he has not the time to expose them all). Then we find the warning given that the monastic practice of feeding the poor was a ploy designed to ensnare them, particularly, '...those needy through their own fault'[13] and he also drags up the Anne Fullard case of ten years earlier, as a 'pious fraud' designed to delude the ignorant. In connection with the 'wicked practices' mentioned above, he claimed that seclusion and retirement were not consistent with either Christian or social duty; he even quotes St John Chrysostom, a fourth century Patriarch of Constantinople, and one of the four doctors of the Eastern Church, to support his argument.

In conclusion he attacked what he saw as the 'worldly dignity' of the monastery buildings and asked ominously 'Does it not savour far too much of earthly dominion and sway?'[14] And he warned people to be on their guard against invitations to public worship and begged them not to go if they were asked, because places of 'Roman schism' were even worse than places of 'Protestant schism'

> 'There can be no fear of the consequences of any solicitations of these kinds to those who are well instructed in the principles of the Christian faith, as taught by the Church of England.'[15]

But the effect of dignified buildings and liturgical pomp on impressionable or ignorant characters could be disastrous. He ended by referring his readers to Articles XX and XXXVII of the Thirty Nine Articles of Religion.[16]

The supplement to this address is what purports to be an eye-witness account of the career of a young nun, who went into a convent to live 'this unnatural and joyless existence'[17] principally it appears because her father's fortune had declined, and 'the convent would require no dower from her'.[18] But having lived in the convent a few months she realises the mistake she was making, and leaves.

The supplement is a comparatively mild attack on the conventual life, and it should be stressed that Merewether confined his opposition to Catholicism strictly within the limits of the reasoned sermon or the written word and would not countenance derogatory abuse or physical violence; and his position, opinions and attitudes exemplify the position of the educated early Victorian of evangelical views not only towards Catholicism, but towards religious enthusiasm in general. Thus in Merewether's supplement, the eyewitness considered the Religious life to be 'a useless and unwholesome state for the young' [19] and concluded with this verdict on monasticism:

'If, "joy shall be in heaven over one sinner that repenteth, more than ninety and nine just persons, which need no repentance", surely those who live in the world, fulfilling their probation in struggling against its manifold temptations, offer a more acceptable sacrifice to God than the poor nun, who even in the exercise of her very virtues, does not violate the gospel precept: "Let your light so shine before men, that they may see your good works, and glorify your Father which is in heaven."' [20]

The Jeffreys case was probably the most spectacular controversy to break over Mount St Bernard in those early years. In January 1849, one William Thomas Jeffreys visited Mount St Bernard and stayed two nights in the guest house. He then left and wrote an account entitled, 'A Narrative of Six Years Captivity among the Monks of St Bernard, Charnwood Forest, Leicestershire', in which he tells how his father, whom he describes as 'an intolerant papist', deserted his wife when she refused to become a Catholic, and came with Jeffreys to Mount St Bernard. There, Jeffreys claimed, he was forced to take vows, and was kept in solitary confinement, starved and beaten. He tells of a monk who tried to escape, being brought back 'his mouth was muffled, his arms tied, and he could make no resistance'. Finally, Jeffreys claimed, after six years of ill-treatment, he managed to escape and made his way to the Methodist Chapel in Loughborough. There a collection was made for him and with this money he went via Leicester to Wednesbury in Staffordshire, where he stayed with the Primitive Methodist minister. Jeffrey's story was printed in May by the former editor of the radical *Birmingham Advertiser* Thomas Ragg. The revelations in Jeffreys' account caused an immediate outcry against Mount St Bernard and caused much ill-will against the Catholic Community in the Midlands. Fr Crewe, a priest from Bilston, quickly wrote a refutation of Jeffreys' claims, but the case had touched a raw nerve of anti-Catholic prejudice which was not to be soothed by reasoned words, particularly if the reasoned words proceeded from a Catholic priest!

Jeffreys was touring from one non-conformist audience to another in Staffordshire and Northamptonshire telling his tale. He even got his audience to provide him with a body-guard as well as money, by claiming that the monks from Mount St Bernard were searching for him and planned to carry him back to the Monastery. Unfortunately for Jeffreys, his tale had a tendency to become increasingly elaborate every time he told it, and it was this tendency which aroused Ragg's suspicions. Eventually in June 1849, he wrote to Benedict Johnson at Mount St Bernard, who as Prior was acting superior during Palmer's temporary absence, asking for a written refutation of Jeffreys' accusations, so that he could be arrested for libel and the whole affair thoroughly investigated. Johnson hurriedly replied to this request, denying emphatically that Jeffreys had ever been a member of the Community at Mount St Bernard. In a postcript to this letter, Johnson mentions that the story had just broken in Whitwick, and that some of the miners and hosiery workers there had threatened to burn down the Catholic school in Whitwick and blow up the monastery! From the tone of the letter it is obvious that Johnson was very concerned about what might happen because of Jeffreys' accusations.

Johnson then sent one of the Community, Br Alexis, to Birmingham with this letter and the Guest House visitors' book for Ragg to examine, as he still possessed the manuscript copy of Jeffreys' narrative. On comparing the handwriting in the visitors' book with the manuscript, it was found that Jeffreys had entered the Guest House the previous January under the name Francis Augustus Arkwright. Ragg then took Br Alexis to Wednesbury, and on being presented with Jeffreys, Br Alexis said he was prepared to swear under oath that Jeffreys was the man who had called himself Arkwright and who had stayed for two nights at Mount St Bernard the previous January. Armed with a witness and evidence, Ragg had Jeffreys arrested, and an investigation at Mount St Bernard was agreed upon.

The investigation took place on 26 June 1849, and De Lisle, as the local magistrate, chaired the proceedings. The investigation was obviously very interesting to people round about, and in the narrative written up afterwards it is reported that large crowds gathered in the monastery grounds whilst the investigation was proceeding inside. Palmer stated that Jeffreys had arrived in the Guest House claiming he was a relative of Richard Arkwright the Derby industrialist, but that he was in disguise as he had recently become a Catholic to the disgust of his family. Palmer claimed that he had been suspicious of Jeffreys' story and had asked him to leave. The gatekeeper, Br Malachi, said he had seen Jeffreys arrive and leave; one Joseph Alger was produced who said he had been a guest at Mount St Bernard in January, and he corroborated Palmer's evidence. Even the errand boy was produced who said that he too had seen Jeffreys in the Guest House.

Jeffreys was then asked to describe the monks' daily diet; this he could not do. The Brothers were presented to him individually and he was asked to name them; this he could not do. Then he was asked to lead the investigating party to the dormitory and the room where he had been kept in solitary confinement, and he could not do this either. By now it was obvious that Jeffreys was a fraud and as in all good Victorian melodrama the scene ended with the villain breaking down and confessing his guilt. He was then taken back to Wednesbury to await trial. On 30 June Jeffreys was tried at Handsworth Petty Sessions, convicted of obtaining money under false pretences and awarded three months hard labour in Stafford prison.

Thomas Ragg, who had published Jeffreys' original narrative, now printed and circulated four thousand copies of his retraction, 'As some little reparation for the injury we have been the innocent means of inflicting on the Community of Mount St Bernard.' And an indication of the interest the Jeffreys case aroused is given by the fact that J.H. Newman, who was at that time living in Birmingham, refers to it in three letters he wrote in July 1849. He wrote to a Miss M.R. Giberne that:

> 'There has been a vile calumny here against the Mount St Bernard monks, Trappists, from a fellow who said he had been confined there against his will for six years. The people were furious all about, and it was thought the building

would be pulled down — Luckily the fellow was detected and is now in jail. A reaction has ensued and I think even we are reaping he benefit of it. But I wish people would soften towards our doctrines ever so little — it is only a reaction in our favour as persons.'[21]

In a letter to Ragg thanking him for publishing the refutation, Newman made the comment that:

'A Catholic, a Monk, a Jesuit, or a Pope, is a monster, till he is seen and known to be a man with human feelings, a human heart, a conscience, and a love of mankind.'[22]

And in a letter to George Ryder, Manning's relation through marriage and a frequent visitor to Mount St Bernard, Newman said that the affair had ruined the 'Protestant Watchman' a group set up in Birmingham to oppose Popery. It appears that the Watchman had already attacked Newman for failing to respond to an invitation to take part in a public debate.

But the interest shown in the Jeffreys case indicates that anti-Catholic feeling remained strongly ingrained in the English character. It was to burst forth again in the following year over the so-called 'Papal Aggression', when Pius IX restored the Episcopal Hierarchy in England. On that occasion even the Prime Minister, Lord John Russell, agreed with the Bishop of Durham that the Restoration was 'insolent and insidious' and complained that:

'There is an assumption of power in all the documents which have come from Rome; a pretension of supremacy over the realm of England, and a claim to sole and undivided sway, which is inconsistent with Queen's Supremacy, with the rights of our Bishops and clergy, and with the spiritual independence of the nation, as asserted even in Roman Catholic times.'[23]

It was against such attitudes that the English Catholic community had to contend in the first half of the nineteenth century. From the reasoned yet impassioned oratory of Francis Merewether and his like, to the rabble-rousing cries of 'No Popery' anti-Catholicism drew upon two major sources. The first was a theological conviction that Roman Catholicism had perverted and distorted the true doctrine of Christianity. Secondly, on a political level it was believed that the Church sought a position of authoritarian dominance which would not allow freedom of expression or religious dissent. Merewether confined himself primarily to a theological critique of Catholicism, whilst Jeffreys and some of the pamphleteers in the Anne Fullard case appealed to the less edifying instincts inherent in the cry 'No Popery' which resulted during the Jeffreys' case, in the threat from the Whitwick miners to blow up Mount St Bernard.

As will be seen, Gentili and the early missioners all had to cope with this attitude towards Catholicism. Gentili was on occasions attacked and often pelted with mud, being not just a Roman Catholic priest, but a **foreign** Roman Catholic priest, a combination guaranteed to arouse a reaction. But Daniel Defoe in a previous century had aptly summed up the nature of much of this opposition when he wrote that there were:

'ten thousand stout fellows that would spend the last drop of their blood against Popery, that do not know whether it be a man or a horse.'[24]

Given the strength of feeling against Catholicism it is surprising that the missioners were able to work as effectively as they did, quite apart from revealing their conviction and courage. It does perhaps suggest that the forces of anti-Catholicism, although formidable, were not as strong as they might at first appear. In other words when put to the test by Gentili and the missioners, the forces of English anti-Catholicism were found to generate a great deal of smoke with very little fire.

Plate 15: Father Luigi Gentili, 1801-1848

Chapter Five

LUIGI GENTILI AND THE REVIVAL IN THE VILLAGES

If one man can be said to have initiated the Catholic Revival in north-west Leicestershire, that man was Ambrose De Lisle. He it was who made possible the foundation of Mount St Bernard Abbey, and it was he who invited Fr Luigi Gentili of the Institute of Charity (Rosminians) to use Grace Dieu Manor as his Mission centre. The need for priests was urgent: in the Western District, which included the whole of Wales, it was recorded in 1838 that there were approximately twelve thousand Catholics served by only seventy-four priests, and that number included those priests living at Prior Park and Downside Abbey near Bath. Many Catholics in the country areas thought themselves lucky if they heard Mass once a month, and many died without the possibility of a priest in attendance.

De Lisle approached Rosmini, the founder of the Institute of Charity, with the suggestion that Gentili should come to Grace Dieu. Gentili had previously lived at Prior Park, and had acted as Confessor to the Augustinian nuns at Spettisbury near Blandford, before returning to Rome in 1837, where he was made a Presbyter of the Rosminian Order. It was expected that Gentili would then return to Spettisbury, but Rosmini, mindful of De Lisle's request, detained him in Italy, where he taught philosophy at Calvario, and led retreats for Clergy and Religious. De Lisle had given Rosmini the impression that he would start a Rosminian novitate at Grace Dieu where English priests could be trained. As will be apparent later, De Lisle's finances made such an ambitious foundation impossible. De Lisle was burning to further the work of Catholic evangelism in England, and this appears to have been one of the numerous occasions when his enthusiasm got the better of his discretion. It is also obvious that Gentili was very much a second choice, for in January 1839 De Lisle had petitioned the General Chapter of the Passionists to send Dominic Barberi (the famous missionary who has since been beatified) to Grace Dieu. He said that he would provide a house in Leicestershire for six or seven members with Barberi as Superior. Unfortunately for De Lisle Barberi was appointed Provincial of the Northern Province in Italy.

Meanwhile, Rosmini, who knew nothing of this approach to the Passionists, was very enthusiastic about the idea of Gentili going to Grace Dieu, his only qualm was about Gentili living

> 'in the houses of the rich, even though they are holy, and hence it would be better if he could live quietly by himself, or at least eat apart like a poor man.'[1]

But Rosmini appears to have had such trust in De Lisle that he nevertheless allowed Gentili to go and work from Grace Dieu alone. He left Stresa on 5 May 1840, and arrived at Grace Dieu on 12 June. Grace Dieu Manor was built by Charles March Phillipps for his eldest son Ambrose de Lisle, who had moved into it in 1833 on his marriage to Laura Clifford. There were, in the vicinity, the ruins of a medieval Augustinian convent, from which the dower house estate took its name.

His mission field consisted of the four villages of Shepshed, Hathern, Belton and Osgathorpe. Shepshed was by far the largest village with approximately four thousand inhabitants, the vast majority of whom depended for a living on domestic frame-knitting, as did the two thousand inhabitants of Belton and the eight hundred at Osgathorpe. Out of the seven thousand inhabitants of his mission area, Gentili discovered on his arrival that only twenty-seven were Catholics, and twelve of those lived at Grace Dieu Manor; and of the remaining fifteen, none of them actually lived in Shepshed. These Catholics usually worshipped in the Chapel at Grace Dieu, although with the dedication of Mount St Bernard in 1837, some of them attended the public services there and in the same year De Lisle opened a Mass centre in Whitwick. But either way it involved quite a trek across fields or badly made roads to attend the services and Gentili realised that if he was to win converts, he had to provide some means for the Catholics in each community to meet and worship locally. This, as will be seen, was to become a bone of contention with De Lisle, who wished to retain the Chapel at Grace Dieu as the centre of Catholic worship. The isolation of Grace Dieu was also to become a problem for Gentili. Initially he welcomed the Catholic atmosphere of the Manor; De Lisle was very keen to encourage the work and High Mass was celebrated every Sunday with plainsong sung by a trained choir. But as Gentili wrote to Rosmini in July 1840,

> 'as far as I can see from what I now know, there is not much hope for winning souls. This chapel stands right in the country, and there are three villages round it between two and four miles distant. Here, what with the processions and all other ceremonies that Phillipps has introduced (and I have no hope of cutting them down), there is little time for preaching.'[2]

It was also discovered that De Lisle's income which, because it was derived from a small allowance from his father and from rents which came in only at certain times of the year, and which were static if not falling slowly due to the depression which hit the area in the late 1830s, was not large enough to establish a Mission centre in the area, which had been the original intention. So Gentili had to proceed alone, although he worked on occasions with the monks at Mount St Bernard and with Fr Whittaker at Whitwick, who had recently established a mission aimed at the mining communities which had recently been established on the North West Leicestershire coalfields. But usually Gentili worked alone, walking from Grace Dieu to the villages to preach and teach, and his observations throw a revealing light on the Charnwood district in the early 1840s.

The overwhelming impression was one of poverty and destitution caused mainly be the depressed state of the domestic knitting industry. The hosiery and woollen trades had for centuries been the principal industrial activity of the villages situated in the shadow of Charnwood Forest, hence the name Sheepshead; and that system was essentially domestic. A family would rent one or more knitting frames from a merchant who would also provide raw materials; this was then spun and made up into stockings or whatever garment was required and the merchant paid wages on a piece-work basis. In times of prosperity, such as during the Napoleonic Wars, this system was reasonably successful in that the frame-knitter preserved a measure of independence, working in his own home and regulating his own hours. Thus in 1812 there were nine hundred stocking frames in use in Shepshed which made it, outside Nottingham and Leicester, the major rural centre of the industry. Unfortunately frame-knitting was not a skilled occupation; it was very easy to rent a frame and teach yourself how to use it, with the consequence that when one industry was depressed, as happened in agriculture in this period when the shift from arable to pasture farming forced people off the land, those displaced flocked into the frame-knitting industry, which created a glut of surplus labour which in turn forced down wages. Thus the early 1840s were a time of great distress both in agriculture and the hosiery industry which was a primary factor in the Chartist agitation which occurred at this time in Loughborough and Leicester.[3] As Gentili wrote to Pagani in August 1842 after he had moved to Loughborough:

> 'Lord Shrewsbury has withdrawn into his castle and fortified it with cannon and armed men. Mr Phillipps' father last week was obliged to rush to Shepshed an hour after midnight to read the Riot Act, and was attacked with stones, so that he had to send here to Loughborough for soldiers to escort him home, and his policeman was seriously wounded. Here at Loughborough the soldiers have had to stand-to under arms, to disperse the crowds that collected from all the villages, and the news that comes from the whole district is bad. Thank God we have not been molested except for crowds of poor who come fifty at a time, and it means giving them all bread.'[4]

The missioners arrived in the middle of all this agitation and poverty and what Gentili saw scandalised him. He described the poor as slaves and said that he had never seen poverty like it, even in the Papal States, which at the time was generally considered to be the most poverty stricken, corrupt and badly-governed state in Europe. In January 1841 he wrote to Rosmini:

> 'Not to be able to help these poor people is for me a great trial. Many cannot come to the Chapel to be received or to receive the Sacraments or hear Mass, because they have no shoes, no hats, no decent clothing as they are in rags and half-naked. Then those who have been received into the fold of the Church have no books to use...they come to the Mass, that is those few who can, but without any books, they remain without the spiritual comfort that they need. I do all I can, but without any help I cannot go on, and sometimes the devil tempts me to deep discouragement. The ignorance and vice of these people are such as to beggar description, and the destitution such that I cannot think of it without tears of compassion.'[5]

Earlier the same month he had written to Anna Bolangaro, a benefactor of the Rosminian Order that:

> 'Poverty meanwhile is increasing at an alarming rate. Business is at a standstill, the better class families are in debt, and no one can guess how it will all finish. ...Just to tell you one result, some were put in prison for the Christmas festivities because they did not have the two or three shillings for the Poor Rate; yet they are so poor that they have neither bread nor clothes.'[6]

But it was to his brother that Gentili readily unburdened himself. In a letter to him of May 1841 he mentioned that in one week three people in the villages had committed suicide 'because they could not find anything to eat'[7] and writing again to his brother, a year later he says:

> 'See how God punishes this nation in this area for the last three hundred years. Look at their ignorance, the dense darkness of their minds, the vices that possess them, and then their lack of faith and their poverty, destitution, diseases, humiliations; yet at the same time look at their blind and idiotic pride in four pieces of wood that sails over the waters, causing trouble in every corner of the globe.'[8]

This last letter is revealing for the light it sheds on Gentili's character and view.

The last point is particularly interesting because in 1839, two months after his arrival in England, he wrote to a friend in Italy giving his impressions of England, and after complaining about the climate and the sorry state of Catholicism, he goes on to tell of the poverty he has seen and the very materialistic atmosphere and says:

> 'People shout at you that they are free, but they are slaves to a nobility that wallows in opulence. This idea of independence which in fact they have not got, acts like a drug and hides from them their temporal and spiritual ruin.'[9]

He never could understand how even in the greatest poverty, English people retained their loyalty to what they liked to believe was their unique sense of liberty and freedom, when in many cases, as Gentili saw immediately, it was only a freedom to starve. It also demonstrates that he saw the economic distress as a direct result of the Reformation, not only in the general sense that the present sufferings were God's punishment for three centuries of heresy, but in the more particular sense that such sufferings were directly attributable to the Protestant ethic which, he said, had replaced the Catholic virtues of obedience, humility and charity, with those of individualism, greed and selfishness. Many who heard this responded favourably to it. It should be noted though, that Gentili never really enjoyed his time in England; his comment to Rosmini after his first visit to London was that 'the devil is here seen enthroned, exercising his tyrannical sway over wretched mortals'.[10] He did not like the climate or the materialism and there also appears to be a sense of frustration when people refused to see what to him were the obvious truths of Catholicism, or to accept his belief that their poverty and distress were a direct result of the Reformation and the Protestant ethic. So, as it is difficult to see the good in people or places one dislikes, Gentili's picture of Charnwood should perhaps be seen with this point in mind.

Chapter Six

THE GRACE DIEU YEARS, 1840-1842

The history of Gentili's time at Grace Dieu is interesting not only in connection with the Catholic Revival, but also to see the way in which he went about building up the Catholic Community. After all, he had been sent to Grace Dieu with the simple instruction to convert as many people as possible, but where was he to start?

It appears that his initial approach was to visit people in their homes, particularly the sick, and he soon persuaded an invalid at Osgathorpe he had met this way to allow his house to be used for catechising seven or eight people who found it difficult to walk to Grace Dieu. He also appears to have accosted people in the streets! Leetham tells the story of the grandmother of the late Canon Hunt, the parish priest in Whitwick for many years, who was stopped by Gentili whilst she was endeavouring to cross a stile, and 'with fire in his eyes, earnestly spoke to her of God and her duty to Him.'[1] Respectable ladies were not used to being presented with such naked examples of enthusiasm, particularly when they were half way across a stile!

Father Robert Cooke of the Missionary Oblates of Mary Immaculate, who succeeded Gentili to the Grace Dieu Mission in 1842, tells, in his memoirs, how the first missioners operated in the villages in the early days. It is worth quoting at some length for the light it throws not only on the activities of the missioners, but also on the attitudes of the people they sought to convert:

'On the arrival of a Father in a village in which there was not perhaps a single Catholic, he commenced a course of visits from cottage to cottage, to announce the sermon which he was to preach that same afternoon on the village green, and to invite the inmates to come and hear it...in the meantime, a small platform of some sort was erected on some convenient spot. As the hour of the sermon drew nigh, numbers of villagers might be seen approaching the place of rendezvous in a serious, thoughtful manner, and in many instances each bore a chair on his or her shoulders for use during the sermon... The subject was always on some great Christian truth, such as salvation, conversion, the passion of Jesus Christ, etc: controversy was avoided. At the close of the sermon expressions of satisfaction and goodwill fell from the lips of several in the crowd, accompanied by invitations to the Father to renew his visit at some early date. Many also, on those occasions, used to express their astonishment that such scriptural doctrines could be preached by a Catholic Priest, as they had always been led to believe that Catholic Priests did not hold with Scripture Truths'.[2]

Another anecdote recounted by Leetham not only indicates how the nucleus of a parish was established in Shepshed, but also of the dangers Gentili and his early converts faced. It appears that a certain Mr Grimley threatened to beat his wife if she did not stop talking to Gentili. Some time after this Gentili was

Plate 16: Shepshed Market Place c.1890

attacked whilst working in Shepshed, and finished up in a ditch with a sprained ankle. Some bystanders then went to the house of Mr Grimley, which was presumably nearby, to get help; he reluctantly agreed to take Gentili in and dress his wounds. The upshot was that Mr Grimley and his wife were converted, and their house became one of Gentili's first centres in the village.

Gentili then persuaded De Lisle to rent a room in one of Shepshed's many public houses, probably in one of the four 'pubs' (known as the Blue Bell, the Bull's Head, the Crown and the Ram), which then graced the Market Place, where he delivered two lectures a week. His audience was soon over a hundred, whom he divided into adults and children and instructed separately; but the numbers kept growing until, with the permission of Bishop Walsh, he began to preach outside in the Market Place. Some indication of the effect of his presence can be derived from the fact that at Christmas 1840, after only six months in the area, he received into the Church fifty adults in the Chapel at Grace Dieu.

In defiance of De Lisle's love of correct liturgical form, Gentili encouraged the use of English in the services and he would often preach in the streets. On one occasion this resulted in his being burnt in effigy at Osgathorpe, and his reply was to stand on the spot the next day and begin his preaching again; to be a missioner demanded courage as well as conviction. In July 1840, Gentili wrote to Miss Frances Taylor of Cannington, Somerset, and mentioned the converts he had under instruction, who would be received in Grace Dieu Chapel the following Christmas, and the fact that all these first converts came from Shepshed. But 'you may easily understand that I have to contend with the most violent opposition from the parsons and their party.'[3] He also claimed that there would be many more converts in Shepshed if there was a Chapel in the village and a Sunday School.

He mentioned that a wealthy Baptist gentleman had built a hall specifically 'for any new sort of religion that would come there'[4] and that the price for the hall was £60. As Gentili was preaching 'a new sort of religion' he approached the owner who agreed to rent it to him. Unfortunately by the following January, Gentili was again writing to Miss Taylor saying that the Baptist gentleman, having become alarmed by the rapid spread for Popery, had withdrawn his offer; so that Gentili was left with a growing congregation and no meeting place.

It was after the failure of these negotiations that land was bought on the corner of Pick Street and Belton Street and a Chapel designed and built by A.W.N. Pugin for £700. Whilst the Chapel was being built Gentili rented a disused Methodist Chapel on Church Street which was used as a temporary Chapel and a poor school. The school remained after the Chapel was opened in Pick Street, until 1852 when the Rosminians left the area. Meanwhile work went ahead on the new Chapel. With his experience of Mount St Bernard, Pugin was a past master of the art of building substantial buildings on a shoestring and St Winefride's, Shepshed must to be the pinnacle of that particular art!

£500 had been raised through subscription and the remaining £200 was donated by John Talbot, Earl of Shrewsbury. The Church was built in less than a year and consecrated by Bishop Walsh on 18 November 1842, and one Fr Signini, a fellow Rosminian missioner, was appointed Priest-in-Charge. In the beginning the priest travelled to Shepshed from Loughborough or stayed in the houses of the laity, but this was obviously an inconvenience for the priest who had a growing congregation to attend to. So in 1844 De Lisle provided them with a house in the 'Flats' and in a letter to Pagani he explains the progress of the alterations which were designed to make it 'quite unnecessary for any female to enter their dwelling'.[5]

In May 1841, De Lisle recorded the following number of converts:

Shepshed	320
Belton	100
Osgathorpe	100
Hathern	50

Unfortunately De Lisle, in his enthusiasm, was inclined to exaggerate, and the figures do not record how many converted out of economic interest, ie how many were tenants or dependants of De Lisle and who were thus influenced. But it does suggest that Gentili and other missioners had aroused interest in the area, although there was much opposition, much playing on traditional anti-foreign as well as anti-Catholic prejudice. Although, compared to the numbers who came to hear Gentili preach, the number of converts was small, nevertheless progress was made, and the presence of Gentili, Cooke and the Mission in Loughborough did begin to undermine the anti-Catholic prejudices, by demonstrating that Catholic priests were human beings and not devils in cassocks.

But where did the early converts come from? Most of Gentili's converts were non-conformists, at least nominally, for the simple reason that most of the lower orders in the Charnwood area had moved away from the Church of England into dissent before Gentili arrived. Thus out of the two thousand inhabitants in Belton in the early 1840s, only about two hundred regularly attended the Parish Church. Leetham in his biography of Gentili argues that the attacks launched upon him from the pulpit of St Botolph's Shepshed, was an element in his sucess in the village. The general feeling appeared to be that whatever the Established Church denounced, was worth looking into. Pagani wrote as follows on the activities of Joseph Hamilton, the Vicar of Shepshed until 1848, and his attitude to the missioners:

Plates 17 & 18: Exterior and Interior of St Winefride's, Shepshed.

'Not satisfied with previously calumniating the Catholic Church from the pulpits of error, they (the Anglicans) also sought out those who had received from Gentili any Catholic books, and took them away. They promised employment, with land to grow potatoes, and held out other advantages to induce them to renounce Catholicity and adhere to Protestantism. The parson of Shepshed, in particular, distinguished himself by his maniacal zeal, and did what he could to prevent parents from permitting their children to attend the Catholic Chapel. He sent emissaries to distribute tracts calculated to excite ridicule against the Catholic belief concerning images, indulgences, prayers for the dead, the real presence, etc. He engaged a curate to assist in opening a school for children, to whom lessons were given to learn at the precise time that Fr Gentili came to give his instructions, and thus they were prevented from hearing him. At the same time also appointed by Gentili for the adults, the parson began to give a no popery lecture.'[6]

However, the 'iniquities' of the Anglican clergy should not be exaggerated. Pagani's life of Gentili was designed primarily as propaganda, thus to expand upon the amount of opposition which the hero successfully overcame only serves to inspire the reader and enhance the reputation of the character being held up for admiration and imitation. Anglican clergymen of the eighteenth and early nineteenth centuries are invariably presented either as well-fed, wine-guzzling, fox-hunting Tories, or as fanatically anti-Catholic bigots. Such a view is necessarily a caricature, as many country clergy in this period were conscientious and hard-working in their parishes. This includes Merewether at Whitwick and Hamilton himself who, despite Pagani's image, established a clothing fund to help the Shepshed poor in the 1840s. At the same time the Oxford Movement was gathering strength, which indirectly encouraged the Church of England to be far more aware of its social responsibilities.

But having said all that it is undoubtedly true that one element in Gentili's success was his ability to cut away many of the social taboos which had grown up within the denominations. Thus he would not allow pew-renting, nor would he take the customary fee for baptising children and the Sunday and Day Schools he started were also free. One interesting insight into social custom of the time was the vexed question of 'Sunday-best'. It has been suggested that one factor in encouraging the poor to attend the Catholic Chapel rather than Anglican or non-conformist worship, was that they could attend Catholic worship without having to wear 'Sunday best' and thus did not feel the discomfort of having to sit at the back and defer to their betters, which was a feature of Anglican and some non-conformist churches. Writing on the habits of English Catholics in this period, Fr P. Hutton, who became President of Ratcliffe College in 1850, remarked on the raw converts predilection for preaching and the importance they attached to having 'Sunday-best'. Both habits, he believed, they had learnt from their Protestant upbringing and neighbours. He writes that:

'This passion for preaching and preachers is so deeply rooted in the national mind that Protestants, to designate what particular place of worship they frequent, or what persuasion they follow, are accustomed to say that they sit under or, in other words, go and hear such-and-such a preacher. The consequence is that if ever they become Catholics, as in the Protestant or Dissenting chapels the principal sermon generally takes place in the evening, nothing is so difficult as to convince, especially the more rude and illiterate, of the necessity of attending Mass on a Sunday morning in preference to the evening service.

Another reason may be that no Protestant, however poor, will think of venturing out on a Sunday without being dressed far above his condition. This circumstance alone renders it very difficult to draw the lower classes out of their houses before the latter part of the day. How often may not the laborious missioner hear the poor female proselyte alleging, as what she considers a most valid excuse for not having come on the previous Sunday to make her public profession and be received into the Church, that bad times, the impossibility of her husband finding any employment, and their consequently distressed circumstances, had compelled her to pawn her best clothes, and it was therefore impossible for her to attend, however much she might wish! And so much shame and obloquy are attached in this country to the circumstances of a person, of however mean condition, appearing in public on a Sunday in poor and homely apparel, far be it from me to pronounce how far this pretext may avail in the sight of heaven! Even the poor and faithful Irishman, after a certain sojourn in this proud and sensual country, becomes more or less affected by the same human respect, from the repeated sneers and taunts of his neighbours. All that I have hitherto said may convey some idea of the nature of missionary life in England.'[7]

Generally speaking, Gentili's converts were amongst those who were of the wrong social class to find a place within the Church of England or the old established non-conformist churches, and who had suffered in the rapid changes in industry. In consequence they had largely renounced their loyalty to Squire and Parson. Yet it was an age which still believed that religion was important. Given such a situation, Gentili, mainly by the force of his personality, was able to break through the English dislike of foreigners and the ingrained fear and suspicion of anything savouring of Roman Catholicism. Unlike the Anglican clergy, he visited the sick and aged, preached in the open air, talked to people as people rather than as cogs in the social hierarchy, and emphasised their duty to God rather than their duty to maintain the established order. He told them their sufferings were a result of the Reformation, and it was a message which appealed to many.

★

It has already been noted in connection with the founding of Mount St Bernard, that De Lisle envisaged Grace Dieu Manor as being the centre of the Catholic Mission in the Charnwood area. De Lisle still saw himself in the pre-Emancipation role as the leading Catholic landowner in the area, who was in effect the leader of the local Catholic community. Gentili complained that this attitude in effect dictated to the Hierarchy and hampered the work the missioners were trying to do. This theoretical difference over the position of the Gentry and the Hierarchy affected their relationship. Gentili complained that De Lisle used him as a private chaplain, and that he was obliged to spend far too much time in ceremonial and processions in the Chapel at Grace Dieu. Unlike De Lisle, who saw Grace Dieu as the hub of Catholicism in Charnwood, Gentili saw it very much as a starting point, and that he himself was a missionary priest not a private chaplain dependent on De Lisle's favour. The differences between De Lisle and Gentili indicate the change that came over English Catholicism after the Emancipation. Catholicism was emerging from the private chapels of the Gentry and a new and far more vigorous spirit began to show through. The Gentry saw their influence declining as Priests became obedient to the Bishops rather than dependent on themselves, and the differences between De Lisle and Gentili at Grace Dieu occurred in private chapels all over the country at this time.

The actual break between De Lisle and Gentili came in May 1842. Whilst the Chapel was being built in Shepshed, Gentili had obtained Bishop Walsh's permission to celebrate Mass in the house of a convert in Shepshed. De Lisle was not enthusiastic about this because if Shepshedians heard Mass in Shepshed rather than at Grace Dieu then the congregation there would be smaller. To make up the numbers De Lisle proposed that Whitwick should become part of Gentili's 'parish' so that the Catholics from Whitwick would have to go to Grace Dieu to hear Mass. Gentili objected to this because he thought it was unfair on Fr Whittaker, the missioner in Whitwick, to change in so arbitrary a fashion his area of work. De Lisle then appears to have lost his temper and forbade Gentili to say Mass in Shepshed. Gentili retorted that he had the Bishop's permission, and that the people needed it; whereupon De Lisle sacked him as his chaplain. Gentili then left Grace Dieu and moved into the Rosminian Mission house in Loughborough, where he was to stay for another two years. His place at Grace Dieu was taken by Robert Cooke and the Missionary Oblates of Mary Immaculate who stayed until 1848. De Lisle and Gentili continued to meet and work together after this, as Gentili was to be instrumental in establishing a Calvary at Grace Dieu shortly afterwards, but on a basis of equality rather than as Squire and private chaplain.

Chapter Seven

GENTILI IN LOUGHBOROUGH 1842-45

In 1824 a priest from Birmingham, Fr Thomas McDonnell, came to Loughborough to visit a young man who had requested instruction in the Catholic faith; his name was Ambrose De Lisle. They met in the house of an Irishwoman somewhere in Loughborough, whose house appears to have been used by the few Catholics of the area as a meeting place. The following year McDonnell returned and received De Lisle into the Church in the house of an Irish paviour. The next record of a priest being in Loughborough is four years later in 1829 when Fr William Hopkins baptised a child at the small meeting place which the Catholics used above an ironmonger's shop in Market Street, or Mill Street as it was then called.

Neither Fathers McDonnell or Hopkins were resident in Loughborough, the few Catholics being dependent on the rare visits of priests from Leicester or Birmingham. In 1831 an Irishwoman from Loughborough took her child to Holy Cross Priory in Leicester to be baptised and presented it to Fr Benjamin Hulme, a convert from Anglicanism who had only recently been ordained. When Hulme discovered there was no resident priest or permanent Church in Loughborough he wrote to Bishop Walsh of the Midland District asking permission to establish a Mission in Loughborough. Walsh complied and Hulme arrived in Loughborough early in 1833 and stayed with an Irishman, McElroy, in his public house on Ashby Road. The first Masses were said in the homes of the faithful. Hulme then set about raising the money for a Church and raised £5,000 through subscriptions and donations, quite a sum in the early 1830s! To avoid controversy Hulme bought a plot of land on Ashby Road through an intermediary, but there was a lively exchange of pamphlets when it was discovered that a Catholic chapel was to be built there. However, despite the controversy, the building went ahead and within the year the Church was completed in the Italianate style and dedicated to St Mary.

The baptismal register records sixty-eight baptisms by Hulme in the five years he was at St Mary's and the thirty-eight families entered reveal the significance of the Irish connection. Loughborough's Catholic community, unlike the other villages in the Charnwood area, was based firmly on Irish immigrants. Hulme had increased his congregation from six to around two hundred by the time he left Loughborough in 1839. In an early history of St Mary's it records that Fr Hulme was a popular preacher who attracted many non-Catholics to his sermons, but in those days of fierce religious and inter-denominational controversy Hulme sided with the non-conformists in the agitation to abolish the Church rate, which was a rate levied on each household in a parish and used for the maintenance of the Parish Church. This naturally upset Loughborough's Anglicans and caused such controversy that eventually Hulme asked Bishop Walsh's permission to leave. Thus in 1839 he left Loughborough for the Mission at Newcastle-under-Lyme where he stayed for a short time before moving to Aston Hall, the Passionist's house in Derbyshire.

Hulme's place appears to have been taken by Norbert Woolfrey and Fr George Moclare from Mount St Bernard, as the only entries in the baptismal register at St Mary's between November 1838 and April 1841 were made by Woolfrey and Moclare. Woolfrey was also in charge of the Mission at Barrow-on-Soar during this time. He had gone there in 1839 to answer a 'No Popery' campaign, and as a result of his work there gained enough converts to start a Mission. The Catholic Church at Barrow was built by Irish 'navvies' who were working on the Midland Counties Railway. Thus was the Cistercian Rule of stability and silence adapted during the foundation period to cope with increasing congregations and the lack of priests.

In May 1841 the Loughborough Mission was taken over by Fr Pagani, English Provincial of the Rosminian Order, he was joined by six Irish priests who were training as missionaries for Australia. The Mission consisted of the Chapel, capable of seating three hundred, a house and four adjacent cottages. Pagani added a kitchen and refectory to the house, and knocked the cottages into one; his intention was to start a Rosminian novitiate, but this plan was later transferred to Ratcliffe College.

Gentili arrived from Grace Dieu during the summer of 1842, and Pagani, whose health had never been strong, returned to Italy (he later settled permanently at Oscott House near Birmingham). Meanwhile the ever active Gentili had been busy introducing some distinctly continental practices into Loughborough. He started the Confraternity of the Heart of Mary, a lay organisation which, amongst other things, accompanied pauper funerals to the workhouse cemetery. He later caused a cross to be set up in this cemetery, which eventually became a Catholic burial ground. Inevitably, there was opposition. In a letter to Rosmini, Gentili tells how:

> 'A very wealthy lady of this place (Loughborough) went through all the villages a few days ago throwing handbills attacking us from her carriage; the result is that people are getting more and more incensed against the Anglicans.'[1]

Gentili also established a Catholic Temperance Society in Loughborough and Shepshed which often worked alongside the Protestant Society. But even here there was to be trouble, as Gentili, committed as he was to his missionary work, could not resist using the Temperance platform as a pulpit. This led one non-conformist Minister to complain that:

> 'instead of sticking to the subject of Temperance, he had spent his time in craftily presenting papistical doctrines to his audience.'[2]

This, combined with well attended evening sermons at St Mary's, funeral processions, singing and preaching in the streets, underlined the fears of the militant Protestants, and the early alliance with the Protestant Society over temperance was short-lived. The result was a hardening of anti-Catholic feeling; the Duke of Rutland lent his name to the Loughborough Protestant Society, Catholic shopkeepers were boycotted and many eventually only provided a service for their co-religionists; Catholic employees were dismissed and tenants evicted.

Yet the Catholic population grew slowly, aided in these early years by the hard work and dedication of the Missioners of St Mary's, led by Gentili, who sometimes even broke the law in their desire to help those who came to them. Thus Gentili was nearly imprisoned for performing marriages in an unlicensed building for those who could not afford to buy a marriage licence. He was denounced by the Board of Guardians to the Home Office, but De Lisle had

Plate 19: Interior of St Mary's, Loughborough

asked Lord John Manners, Laura De Lisle's uncle, who was an Under-Secretary of State, to intervene in the case. This string-pulling was successful and the Home Office suspended the charge. Gentili began to hold retreats, and in the two years he was in Loughborough many members of the English Hierarchy made their retreat at the Mission House. He also developed the idea of preaching missions, his first lasted a fortnight and by all accounts was quite a success, bringing nearly one hundred and forty converts, and attended by the Vicar Apostolic of the York District.

But the most lasting development to emerge from the Rosminian Mission in Loughborough was the establishment of a Rosminian convent. It was the ambition of Lady Mary Arundell, a forceful lady who was an enthusiastic supporter of Pagani, the English Provincial. When Pagani came to Loughborough, in 1839, Lady Arundell followed and installed herself at Paget House in Woodgate where she received the first nuns in 1843, Sisters Mary Francesca and Mary Anastasia who were sent by Rosmini from Italy. Their journey from Domodossola in northern Italy to Loughborough, escorted by Fathers Furlong and Hutton, took eleven days including a rough crossing from Ostend to London Docks, during which Furlong was the first to succumb to seasickness. In Loughborough they were received by Pagani and Gentili before moving into Paget House.

Soon after the two Italian Sisters had settled in at Paget House they were joined by one Mrs Lockhart. She was the mother of William Lockhart who had joined Newman in his small community at Littlemore and had been received into the Catholic Church by Gentili at Loughborough in 1843. Mrs Lockhart had also become a Catholic and now presented herself at Paget House as a postulant. Conditions at Paget House were far from luxurious and Sr Mary Francesca ruled her small community with a firm hand. This was unacceptable to an English lady such as Mrs Lockhart who had been used to a comfortable life and to being in charge, so she left and tried to establish another Rosminian House near Greenwich. Apparently the problem of the conditions at Paget House affected others besides Mrs Lockhart for Gentili recorded in his journal that:

> 'Many came to the convent but did not stay, unable to accommodate themselves to the hardships of an unheated house, to the Italian cooking and the unsubtle direction given them by the estimable ladies who did not understand them.'[3]

Most of the English postulants came from 'good' families, such as Mary Amherst who came from a wealthy family. She was a niece of Lord Shrewsbury at Alton Towers, and the austerities at Paget House were, in Gentili's opinion, unsuitable for England. Mary Amherst, who as Sr Mary Agnes, became Superior in 1852, records the impression of gloom at Paget House which she visited in the early 1840s, as she told Gentili at the time 'I have, I must confess, great fear and horror of melancholy nuns.'[4] As an interesting glimpse into the Rosminian Mission, Gentili was also complaining at this time of the terrible food which was served at the Convent and to the novitiate at Ratcliffe College. It was, he thought, an unnecessary austerity which only succeeded in deterring people who wanted to go there on retreat. However, the influence of the austerities in deterring postulants from Paget House should not be over emphasised. All religious communities practice a measure of austerity as part of the discipline of the religious life, and Lady Arundell and her two Sisters were trying to launch a new convent and run a school on very slender resources. Also Mrs Lockhart was trying to establish her own Community at Greenwich, and she tried to attract for it some of the postulants from Paget House.

Plate 20: Mary Amherst (Mother Mary Agnes), founder and first Superior of the Convent of Our Lady, Loughborough.

During this testing early period there occurred a clash between Gentili and Sr Mary Francesca, both Italians and both imbued with great energy and dedication. Sr M. Francesca objected to what she considered Gentili's interference in their diet and life style. She also took exception to his correspondence with the postulants, such as Mary Amherst, whom she thought should put themselves under her guidance as Superior and not Gentili's. The clash between Sr M. Francesca and Gentili appears to have the qualities of an irresistable force meeting an immovable object! Finally, Sr M. Francesca wrote to the authorities in Rome concerning Gentili, who was promptly ordered to break all contacts with the Convent and discontinue his correspondence with the postulants. This was quite a blow to Gentili, but he obeyed and the Convent remained with only two sisters until 1846, after Gentili had left Loughborough, when Mary Amherst, or Sister Mary Agnes as she now was, returned to Loughborough together with Emily Cachard who, as Sr Mary Joseph, succeeded Mary Amherst as Superior in 1860, and Annette Vavasour. Meanwhile the Greenwich house, which Mrs Lockhart had attempted to found, had failed and many came from there to Loughborough, some to complete their postulancy under Sr Mary Agnes. In 1852 Sr Mary Francesca stepped down as Superior. The following year she returned to Italy and Sr Mary Agnes was appointed Superior at the age of twenty-eight. Sr Mary Anastasia remained in Loughborough until her death.

The raison d'etre of Rosminian Sisters was to teach, and as soon as the Italian Sisters arrived at Paget House in 1843, Lady Arundell opened a school. They took in girls as boarders who stayed in the House and started Loughborough's first poor school in the stables for day pupils. In Italy the Rosminian Sisters had travelled the country setting up poor schools where they had taught reading, writing and the catechism, but Gentili considered that the well-bred girls who had so far come forward as postulants would never stand the strain of travelling the country, in the British climate, teaching in poor schools, and, and he wrote to Rosmini suggesting that a static school for girls be established in Loughborough served by the Convent. Rosmini, who probably did not appreciate conditions in England, rejected this suggestion as being incompatible with the spirit of the Rosminian Order. Because of this the Sisters maintained the school at Paget House and also taught in the poor schools at Shepshed, Whitwick and at Turrylog, the school the De Lisle's started near Grace Dieu, as well as in the Sunday schools. These schools were very popular, probably because they were free and the children were provided with a uniform. Many parents felt that the opportunity of free education outweighed the fact that the Catholic catechism was taught. A feature of these day schools, introduced by Gentili, was the annual Prize Giving, a practice he had witnessed in Rome. These were also very popular and one such event in Shepshed attracted over a thousand people.

The school at Paget House continued to grow, and, despite Rosmini's complaints, established itself as a permanent day and boarding school. In 1851 the poor school moved to Gray Street in Loughborough, adjacent to the new convent building into which the Sisters had moved the previous year. By 1850 the community under Sr M. Francesca had grown to around twenty and the new Convent, designed in the Gothic style by Charles Hansom, a disciple of Pugin's, was built on Park Road to accommodate them and the boarders. Thus by 1852 when Sr Mary Agnes became Superior the Convent was firmly established in new purpose-built surroundings, and the boarding school, and the poor school were both flourishing.

It was always one of Gentili's aims to bring the English Catholic Community into accord with Continental Catholicism in respect of practice and outlook. Since the middle of the seventeenth century English Catholicism had been isolated from mainland Europe, thus it had hardly been touched by any influence of the Counter-Reformation and, consequently, was marked by a high level of national autonomy. Most English priests were trained in France and held Gallican views which reduced the power and authority of the Papacy to an absolute minimum. In England, following the Gallican tradition, Catholics distinguished between what they called the Church of Rome, which was a spiritual institution, and the Court of Rome which was seen as a foreign secular power. Thus the Earl of Bristol in 1663 could declare in the House of Commons that:

> 'I am a Catholic of the Church of Rome but not of the Court of Rome; a true Roman Catholic as to the other world, but a true Englishman as to this.'[5]

The Papacy remained as a centre of doctrinal authority but with no secular claims outside the Papal States.

In the eighteenth century English Catholic writers tried to show that it was possible to be a good Catholic as well as a patriotic Englishman. Thus Joseph Barrington, a priest, wrote that Catholics saw the Pope only as first among the Bishops, and in 1789 in a 'Protestation' to Parliament, one thousand five hundred leading Catholics, including three Bishops and two hundred and forty priests, declared themselves to be resolutely opposed to the Pope terminating the allegiance of subjects to the civil power (this refers to the excommunication by Pius V of Elizabeth I which in theory released all Catholics from their allegiance to the Crown, but which in practice left them open to charges of treason) and any notion that the Pope was infallible.

By the beginning of the nineteenth century the English Catholic Community largely ignored the Papacy and had retreated into its own closed world, where they did all they could to hide their Catholicism and practiced their religion behind closed doors and shuttered windows. When asked to comment on their relations with the Papacy most English Catholics were at pains to stress their loyalty to the Crown and the virtual non-existence of any Papal or foreign influence. Thus in the debate leading up to Catholic Emancipation in 1829, the Vicars-Apostolic declared that:

> 'Neither the Pope, nor any other prelate or ecclesiastical person of the Roman Catholic Church has any right to interfere directly or indirectly in the Civil Government.'[6]

And Daniel Rock, an early Victorian priest, was of the opinion that the Papal authority should be reduced to what was 'barely necessary for communion'.[7] Even as late as 1840 Gregory XV considered the English Vicars-Apostolic to be on the brink of schism. Along with this Gallican attitude to the Papacy went an approach to religious practice which was totally alien and unacceptable to Gentili and Italian missioners. Priests were addressed as Mister instead of Father and wore secular dress so as not to draw attention to themselves. English Catholics shared with their Anglican brethren a horror of enthusiasm which they saw as foreign and a threat to their position.

However, by the end of the 1840s a distinct change had occurred in English Catholics. Since Emancipation they had been allowed to practice their religion openly and this encouraged a more strident approach to their faith. Priests began to wear cassocks, birettas and Roman collars and be addressed as Father. It has already been noted how Gentili encouraged devotion to the Virgin Mary and established the Confraternity of the Heart of Mary. Along with continental practices which came into England were the ideas of Ultramontanism, literally, 'over the mountains', which elevated the authority of the Pope over the national Churches as the only centre of unity and doctrinal inspiration. This was to lead to the definition of Papal Infallibility in 1870.

One of Gentili's major successes in 'Romanising' the English Catholics in this area was to establish a Calvary. In 1843, with help from De Lisle, a large Calvary was erected adjacent to Turrylog School near Grace Dieu. Gentili and Fr Rinolfi, also from the Loughborough mission, led a four day preaching mission in Whitwick which culminated in the dedication of the Calvary at which a crowd, estimated at four thousand, heard Gentili and Ullathorne, then a mission priest in Coventry, preach. Ullathorne wrote that:

> 'to see this public memorial of Faith, displayed thus openly in the very centre of England, for the first time in modern ages, in the midst of the scene of his own labours, seemed, while it closed a past order of things, to open a new era in his missionary life.'[8]

In his three year stay in Loughborough, Gentili had personally baptised nearly five hundred adults and children, he had caused the Calvary to be set up, had witnessed the growth of flourishing Catholic Chapels in Loughborough, Shepshed and Barrow-on-Soar. He also taught and encouraged the postulants who were soon to establish the Convent on a firm footing, and after the ban on correspondence was lifted, he maintained a lively correspondence with the sisters until his death in 1848. He had been instrumental in changing the introverted Gallican attitudes of English Catholics wherever he worked, through the introduction of Continental practices, and the injection of a sense of evangelical enthusiasm, spiced with a touch of Ultramontanism. His premature death in 1848 at the age of forty-seven, brought on by overwork and exhaustion, was a severe loss to the Catholic Church in England.

Chapter Eight

CONCLUSION

David Mitchell, in his study of the Jesuits, has estimated that in 1851 two-thirds of the Catholic population in England were Irish. As has been demonstrated above, it was mainly the Irish poor who, according to Bernard Palmer's figures, were seeking relief at Mount St Bernard in their thousands by the late 1840s. The influx of Irish immigrants was to make a great impression on Catholicism both in England and America, in fact many thought that the words 'Irish' and 'Catholic' were interchangeable. But what is noticeable about the Catholic Revival in Charnwood, is that with the exception of Loughborough, the foundations were laid before the Irish immigrations began in large numbers. Mount St Bernard was permanently established, and the Chapels in Loughborough, Shepshed, Coalville, Whitwick and Barrow-on-Soar were all built by 1843, and the converts gained in this period were largely indigenous. Thus the foundations of the modern Catholic Church in England were not, as is sometimes argued, built entirely upon Irish immigration, although that was to be an important contribution to the spread of Catholicism, but on missionary work amongst the indigenous population.

What is also worthy of note is the fact that the Revival in Charnwood was initiated largely by one person, namely Ambrose De Lisle. Thus it is impossible to discuss the Catholic Revival without discussing personalities. It was De Lisle who settled the Cistercians on Tin Meadow, De Lisle who opened his private Chapel to local Catholics, De Lisle who brought Gentili to Charnwood, De Lisle who provided a home for the Missionary Oblates, De Lisle who, from his limited resources, encouraged the work financially, although the Earl of Shrewsbury was the principal source of finance for Catholic foundations in the East Midlands. But it can be said without exaggeration that without De Lisle the Catholic Revival in the Charnwood area would have been on a very much smaller scale. In that sense the social and economic factors, which were touched upon in the Introduction, namely the alienation of many from the religious and economic establishment, must take second place before the importance of personality in this particular instance.

The importance of De Lisle is indicative of the position of the Catholic gentry as a whole, such as Lord Shrewsbury at Alton and Thomas Weld at Lulworth. Without the Catholic gentry it is doubtful whether Catholicism would have survived at all in England after the Reformation. After 1829 they provided land and money, which ensured that Catholic institutions such as schools and monasteries were placed upon a permanent foundation, and that was essential if the gains made by the missioners were to be retained and expanded upon. But there is also the fact that the Church authorities often refused their patron's wishes when those wishes were thought to be excessive, such as the refusal by Bishop Walsh to allow De Lisle's request for a Chaplain from Mount St Bernard. This was part of the deliberate policy of the Church after Emancipation to free itself from the control of the gentry, whilst retaining their allegiance and services. This policy caused many clashes and many a chaplain to be expelled from private Chapels, as was Gentili in 1842, for refusing the wishes of the patron. But despite that, this policy was pursued with quiet determination by the Church authorities, who were determined to be the masters in their own house.

Whilst the personalities were important in furthering the spread of Catholicism, Francis Merewether stands out not only as an example of those who were deeply suspicious of this sudden reappearance of Catholicism, but also as a fine example of an early Victorian Evangelical. His arguments against Catholicism and Monasticism reflect admirably the 'party line' of conservative Evangelical Anglicanism, basing itself firmly on a fundamentalist interpretation of the Bible, a horror of 'enthusiasm', and an implicit assumption that the primary function of Christianity was one of morality and social control. Merewether also reveals some of the popular assumptions concerning Catholicism which were prevalent at the time, such as the fear that Catholicism was seeking to establish a theocratic regime, and that religious freedom would be denied. Anti-Catholic feeling was never far beneath the surface in early nineteenth century Britain, as is evidenced by the reaction locally to the Jeffreys' case, or the national outcry which greeted the 'Papal Aggression' of 1851. Catholics sometimes appeared to occupy a similar position in England to that of the Jews on the Continent, in that they often became the scape-goats in times of crisis. This was certainly true during the English Civl War in the seventeenth century, when nearly every problem or defeat was blamed on the machinations of Jesuits and 'malignant papists', and this sort of attitude appears to have survived well into the nineteenth century. It should not be forgotten that in 1840 the Gordon Riots were still within living memory, and they were incited primarily by a proposed Roman Catholic Relief Bill. It is interesting to speculate to what extent anti-Catholic feeling was a safety valve in the depressed economy of the 1840s.

One of the advantages of studying the localities is that it often adds the human touch to the process of history. Thus the 1840s can be seen in economic, political, sociological or demographic terms; there is discussion of changes in methods of production, or the effects of a widening world market, or population changes and the effects of a depressed economy. Whilst these approaches are necessary and valid, the study of provincial history can reveal the effects of these abstract developments and principles on individuals. In that sense provincial history can be seen as the necessary corrective to the tendency to view history as the unfolding, whether through 'evolution' or 'revolution', of an abstract, determinist process, wherein the individual is largely ignored. This study suggests that the influence of personality coincides with the larger and more abstract development of events. Thus the personality of Gentili was of tremendous significance in building up the local communities, but he was influenced by the Ultramontane tendencies in the Church; personality and 'determinism' coincide and influence each other.

Gentili, like De Lisle, was the main 'personality' in the Charnwood area, and it is interesting to study the way he contributed to the change in outlook which transformed the post-Emancipation Church in England. Because Catholicism had been so strictly confined to the homes of the Catholic gentry, it had become very introverted, conservative and Gallican. Part of the break away from dependency on the gentry was the process of bringing English Catholicism back into the mainstream of continental practice. Gentili was very enthusiastic to further this process, as is evidenced by his founding of the Confraternity of the Heart of Mary, and the setting up of the Calvary at Grace Dieu. Devotion to the Virgin Mary was to be one of the major innovations the Missioners sought to foster, thus the Missionary Oblates who stayed at Grace Dieu between 1842 and 1848 were dedicated to 'Mary Immaculate' years before the doctrine of the Immaculate Conception was promulgated by Pius IX in 1854, together with an attack on Gallicanism and the introduction of a far more militant and Ultramontane view of Church government.

These developments grew out of the fact that the Roman Catholic Church, after the defeat of Napoleon, was in a far stronger position than it had been since the seventeenth century. The French Revolution has largely destroyed the Gallicanism of the Enlightened Despots and the great Prince-Bishops of eighteenth century Europe. The Papacy had suffered during the Revolutionary and Napoleonic period, and was regarded by the restored Monarchs of Europe as a fellow martyr in the cause of Absolutism and a vital agent in the fight against Revolution. The Church profited greatly from this return to Legitimacy and the general reaction against the ideas of 1789; and by the time Gentili had arrived in Charnwood, a new spirit of militancy and authoritative evangelism was transforming the Catholic Church in general and the English Church in particular. Thus, one way of approaching the Catholic Revival in the foundation period, and the major conclusion of this study, is to see it in terms of the renewal of Catholic certainty, which was brought into an area of alienation and disillusionment. Unwittingly, Gentili, the missioners and the whole post-Emancipation Church found themselves in a situation of great potential which they had the personality to exploit.

Appendix

APPENDIX I

English Communities which came from France and Belgium during the French Revolution.[1]

Men

Cistercian (Trappist)	Lulworth (Dorset)
English Benedictines	Acton Burnell (Shropshire)
Jesuits	Stonyhurst (Lancashire)

Women

Benedictine Nuns	Winchester Hammersmith Murnhull (Dorset) Preston (Lancashire)
Canonesses of St Augustine	Hengrave (Suffolk)
Canonesses of the Holy Sepulchre	Holme Hall (Yorkshire)
Carmelite Nuns	Lanherne (Cornwall) Bishop Auckland (Co. Durham) Acton
Dominican Nuns	Hartpury Court (Gloucestershire)
Franciscan Third Order Regular Sisters	Winchester
Poor Clares	Haggerton Hall (Northumberland) Britwell (Oxfordshire)

APPENDIX II

The Articles of Religion referred to by Merewether

Article XX: Of Purgatory

'The Romish Doctrine concerning Purgatory, Pardons, Worshipping and Adoration, as well of Images as of Reliques, and also invocation of Saints, is a fond thing vainly invented and grounded upon no warranty of Scripture, but rather repugnant to the word of God.'

Article XXXVII: Of the Civil Magistrates

'The King's Majesty hath the chief power in the Realm of England, and other his Dominions, unto whom the chief Government of all Estates of this Realm, whether they be Ecclesiastical or Civil, in all cause doth appertain and is not, nor ought to be, subject to any foreign jurisdiction.

Where we attribute to the King's Majesty the chief government, by which Titles we understand the minds of some slanderous folks to be offended; we give not to our Princes the ministering either of God's word or of the Sacraments, the which thing the the Injunctions also lately set forth by Elizabeth our Queen do most plainly testify; but that only prerogative, which we see to have been given always to all godly Princes in holy Scriptures by God Himself; that is that they should rule all estates and degrees committed to their charge by God, whether they be Ecclesiastical or Temporal, and restrain with the civil sword the stubborn and evil-doers.

The Bishop of Rome hath no jurisdiction in this Realm of England...'

APPENDIX III

Letter: De Lisle to Pagani concerning accommodation for priests in Shepshed.[2]

Garendon Park,
November 4th, 1845

My dear Father Provincial,

I enclose to you the accompanying note from Mr Smith the editor of the Laity Directory, from which you will see that he wants a correct list of the Priests as placed in the Missions here at present. Will you have the goodness of giving him the names of the two priests you intend to place at *Shepshed.*

As I mentioned to you the other day, I have finished the alterations in the house at Shepshed so as to make that part which is allotted for the residence of the Priests *perfectly separate* from Fox's House: and though their food will have to be prepared in Fox's house it will be quite unnecessary for any female to enter their dwelling as we have settled with Mrs Fox that her son should wait upon the Priests. The house prepared for them contains two comfortable bedrooms for the Priests, one bedroom for the Lay Brother, and a comfortable sitting room on the ground floor. The house thus prepared they will find very comfortable until the new one is built. Under these circumstances I trust you will be able to carry out your kind promise into execution soon, and if first you have it not in your powers to send a second Priest, I hope you will be able to send the Deacon about whom you spoke to me when you were at Grace Dieu — as *he* might take the *preaching* on Sundays, for that is the Department in which good Mr Crosbie fails, and I fear there is no hope of congregation or of any frequenting of sacraments so long as there is not a preacher who can command attention, or at least who can be understood by the people, which I fear good Mr Crosbie scarcely is. I will not say any more at present as I am in a great hurry: but commending myself to your devout prayers. I am very dear Father Provincial,

Most sincerely yours in Christ
Ambrose Lisle Phillipps

APPENDIX IV

A.P.U.C.

Manifesto of the A.P.U.C. taken from F.G. Lee (ed) *Essays on the Re-Union of Christendom,* London, 1867, pp 298-9

Association for the Promotion of the Unity of Christendom

(Est. September 8th 1857 — Feast of the Nativity of the Blessed Virgin Mary)

An Association has been formed under the above title, to unite in a band of intercessionary prayer members both of the clergy and laity of the Roman Catholic, Greek and Anglican Communions. It is hoped and believed that many however widely separated at present by their religious convictions, who deplore the grievous scandal to unbelievers, and the hindrances to the promotion of truth and holiness among Christians, caused by the unhappy divisions existing amongst those who profess to have 'One Lord, One Faith, One Baptism', will recognise the consequent duty of joining their intercession to the Redeemer's dying prayer, 'that they all may be One, as Thou, Father, art in me, and I am in Thee, that they also may be one in us, that the world may believe that Thou has sent me.' To all, then, who while they lament the divisions among Christians, look forward to their healing mainly to a corporate reunion of those three great bodies which claim for themselves the inheritance of the priesthood and the name of Catholic, an appeal is made. They are not asked to compromise any principles which they rightly or wrongly hold dear. They are simply asked to unite for the promotion of a high and holy end, in the reliance in the promise of Our Divine Lord, that 'whatsoever we shall ask in prayer believing, we shall receive.' and that 'if two or three agree on earth as touching anything that they shall ask, it shall be done for them of My Father who is in heaven.' The daily use of a short form of prayer together with an 'Our Father' — for the intention of the Association is the only obligation incurred by those who join it; to which is added in the case of priests, the offering, at least once in three months, of the Holy Sacrifice, for the same intention.

Form of Prayer

Lord Jesus Christ, who saidst unto Thine Apostles, Peace I leave with you, My Peace I give unto you; regard not my sins, but the faith of Thy Church; and grant Her that Peace and Unity which is agreeable to Thy Will. Who livest and reignest, God for ever and ever. Amen.

Our Father, etc.

Note: In joining the Association, no one is understood as thereby expressing an opinion on any matter which may be deemed a point of controversy or on any religious question except that the object of the Association is desirable.

Those who are desirous of joining the Association are requested to write out the declaration printed in italics below, append to it their name and place of residence in full and return it to the General Secretary of the A.P.U.C., care of Mr J.T. Hayes, Lyall Place, Eaton Square, London S.W.

Declaration

I willingly join the A.P.U.C., and undertake (in case of clergy: to offer the Holy Sacrifice once in three months) and to recite daily the above prayer for the intention of the same

signed......................................

N.B. the names of members will be kept strictly private.

(Translations of the above were then given in Latin, French, Italian and Greek)

The A.P.U.C. was, for its time, a remarkable association, which is important in view of the present interest in ecumenism. But, if the A.P.U.C., founded on 8 September 1857 with De Lisle as one of the founder members, is remarkable, even more remarkable from the point of view of early ecumenism is the following letter sent by the monks of Mount St Bernard to J.R. Bloxam (1807-1891) one of the early supporters of the Oxford Movement and a close friend of J.H. Newman, in February 1841:

'The Cistercian Brethren of the Monastery of Mount St Bernard to the Reverend Clergy of the ancient Anglican Church, residing at Oxford and elsewhere, health and happiness, grace and eternal salvation.

Reverend and most beloved Brethren in Jesus Christ.

Blessed be God and the Father of our Lord Jesus Christ, the Father of mercies and God of all consolation, who comforteth us in all our tribulations.

It has been a source of unspeakable joy to our hearts, to learn that you most beloved Brethren, being adjusted by your profound learning, love of venerable antiquity, great sincerity and an ardent thirst for truth; having thoroughly searched the Scriptures and the writings of the Holy Fathers; having thereby been brought to the conviction, that many holy practices and doctrines of the ancient Catholic Church, and which were indeed held in veneration by the primitive Anglican Church, are still worthy of your veneration and practice. Hence, most beloved Brethren in Jesus Christ, we cannot but entertain the very consoling hope and the enchanting anticipation that this speedy and laudable retrogression you are making towards the boundaries of venerable antiquity will in long sweetly unite you and us together in one. And "Oh! how delightful it is for brethren to dwell together in one." What is more natural than that we should be rejoiced, that we should superabound with holy joy, at such a charming prospect of our speedy reunion? "For God is our witness how we desire you in the bowels of Jesus Christ." Are we not brethren in Christ, fellow countrymen, and do we not all hope to be lovingly united in the bosom of God for endless ages? Oh! then, in the name of the God of love let hostilities cease, let there be sweet reconciliation, a perfect union. Too long alas have we been separated, to long estranged from one another. From henceforth let there be peace and charity which is the bond of perfection.

May the God of love, to whom we incessantly offer up our most fervent supplications for the consummation of this most desirable reunion, be pleased in his tender mercy to remove all obstacles; and inspire the authorities of the Catholic Church to grant you every possible concession that you may reasonably desire; and thus hasten the dawning of that blessed day, when you and we shall kneel before the same altar, and with one heart and one mind adore the Father of mercies in spirit and truth.

That the grace of our Lord Jesus Christ and the communication of the Holy Ghost may ever be with you all, Most Beloved Brethren.

The devout and humble prayer of your devoted Friends in Christ and humble Servants,

Priests:
Brother Bernard John Palmer, Prior
Brother Odilo William Woolfrey, Sub-Prior
Brother Benedict Joseph Johnson, Master of Novices

Brother Stephen Francis Hawkins, Housekeeper
Brother Edmund Francis Moore, Guest Master
Brother Joseph John Dunne
Brother Benedict John Murphy
Brother Aloysius Henry Tatchell
Brother Andrew Joseph Cornall
Brother Francis Nicholas Murphy
Brother Xavier William Johnson
Brother Luke Levermore
Brother Ignatius Cornelius Boardman
Brother John McDonnell
Brother Placidus Cornelius Boardman
Brother Augustine William Higgs
And the rest.'[3]

This early concern for cooperation between Catholicism and Anglicanism continued with many close connections with the developments at Oxford which later came to be known as the Oxford Movement. De Lisle demonstrated great concern for unity throughout his life and received many of the Oxford men at Grace Dieu and with Gentili, De Lisle visited Oxford in 1842, where they met Newman at Littlemore, the small house where Newman hoped to reintroduce the Monastic life into the Church of England. Thus the foundation of the A.P.U.C. in 1857 had been preceded by many years of contact between De Lisle, the Community at Mount St Bernard and the Oxford Movement.

The A.P.U.C. began with fourteen founder members of which nine were Anglicans, one a Russian Orthodox priest, and the remaining four Catholics. The four Catholic members included, along with De Lisle, Fr Austin Collins (1827-1919) who was Chaplain at Grace Dieu (1859-1861) before entering Mount St

Bernard where he retained his interest in ecumenism and encouraged De Lisle in his ideas of a Uniate Church after the A.P.U.C. had been condemned by Pius IX. The principal Anglican member was Dr F.G. Lee, Vicar of All Souls, Lambeth who was a well-known member of the 'Ritualist' Party in the Church of England and became a Catholic on his death-bed.

But even before the Association was formed the Catholic authorities were suspicious of the intentions and doubtful as to its orthodoxy. In September 1857 two months before the A.P.U.C. was formally launched, Wiseman told De Lisle that the Roman authorities would never accept the ecumenical aims of the A.P.U.C., and in June of the same year the Bishop of Southwark had written to Cardinal Barnabo, head of Propaganda in Rome, criticising an article De Lisle had written entitled 'on the future Unity of Christendom' because it was not sufficiently ultramontane, nor did it reiterate the unique truth of Roman Catholicism against other denominations. It was essentially these two points which were to lead to the condemnation in 1864.

Although Roman Catholic participation in the A.P.U.C. was to lead to censure from Rome, nevertheless for a while a great deal of enthusiasm was shown towards the A.P.U.C. in certain Catholic circles; as De Lisle wrote to Lord John Manners:

> 'We soon counted among our ranks many Catholic bishops and archbishops and dignitaries of all descriptions from Cardinals downwards; the Patriarch of Constantinople and other great Eastern prelates, the Primate of the Russian Church...I do not think any Anglican bishops joined us, but a large number of clergy of the second order.'[4]

Masses were offered at Mount St Bernard and at Grace Dieu for the success of the Association and in 1860 F.G. Lee and the Anglican Bishop of Brechin, who was interested in the work of the A.P.U.C. although his position meant that he could not openly be a member, attended the dedication of the Chapter House at Mount St Bernard, along with other A.P.U.C. members.

The work of the A.P.U.C. based as it was around the commitment to daily prayer and, for priests, a celebration of the Eucharist in the name of unity at least once every three months, was mainly that of meeting with and exploring other Christian traditions with a view to breaking down the barriers which existed between denominations. This was based on the assumption that the Anglican, Orthodox and Roman Catholic Churches were equally valid branches of the Universal Church, separated by accidents of history; and it was to be on this point that A.P.U.C. clashed with the Roman authorities.

In April 1864, Ullathorne, Bishop of Birmingham, wrote to Barnabo at Propaganda concerning A.P.U.C., Barnabo referred the matter to the Holy Office. In June a letter arrived at Propaganda from Cardinal Manning strongly criticising *The Union*, the paper of the A.P.U.C. and its editor. This criticism from two of the most respected members of the English Hierarchy, coupled with the recommendation of the Holy Office, resulted in the publication on 16 September of the Papal Rescript *Ad Omnes Episcopes Anglise* which condemned A.P.U.C. because it subverted the divine constitution of the Church, it presupposed the validity of Churches not in communion with the See of Rome, and implicitly denied that the Roman Church, as it stood, was the only true Church of Christ; arguing that the true Church consisted partly of the Church of Rome and 'partly also of the Photian Schism (Eastern Orthodox) and the Anglican heresy, to which equally with the Roman Church belong the One Lord, the One Faith and the One Baptism' (*Ad Omnes...* 16.9.64). In the countdown to the Vatican

Council of 1870 which was to define Papal Infallibility, Pius IX was not going to allow A.P.U.C. to dilute Catholicism by suggesting that the Church of Rome did not hold a monopoly of the truth.

De Lisle was bitterly disappointed by the reaction of the Roman Authorities, and in December 1864 Manning wrote to Mgr Capalti, Secretary of Propaganda, telling him that the Catholic reunionists intended to appeal to Cardinal Patrizi at the Holy Office against the Rescript. But the publication during December of the Syllabus of Errors and the encyclical *Quanto Cura* frustrated any hope of appeal; and on 20 December De Lisle resigned from the A.P.U.C., complaining to the editor of *The Union* that 'the authorities had been deceived by a false relation of fact', but that he resigned 'under protest, as an act of submission to the Holy See.'[5]

The history of the A.P.U.C. after the publication of *Ad Omnes* in September 1864, was to be one of continual rejection by the Roman authorities. In June 1865 the Anglican members of the A.P.U.C. appealed to Rome against the exclusion of the Catholic members and received a reply from the Holy Office which said in effect that Roman Catholicism held an absolute monopoly of truth, which meant that any Church not in full Communion with Rome was heretical; and ended with an appeal to the Anglican reunionists to abjure heresy and become Roman Catholics. This attitude was further underlined by the failure of A.P.U.C. to win recognition at the Vatican Council in 1870, and by the publication in 1899 by Leo XIII of the encyclical *Apostolicae Curae,* which declared Anglican ordination to be invalid. This uncompromising stance taken by the Holy See effectively barred any ecumenical activity by or with Catholics; and although contacts between Anglicans and Orthodox remained, the purpose of the A.P.U.C. had been effectively undermined and it disbanded in 1921.

After the condemnation of A.P.U.C. and De Lisle's subsequent resignation, he turned his attention to the formation of an English Uniate Church, by which the Church of England would be in full communion with the Holy See, but retain its vernacular liturgy and practices, based upon the Book of Common Prayer. This scheme demonstrates De Lisle's determination to further the cause of Christian unity, but it is doubtful if the idea would have generated much enthusiasm within Anglican circles. Nevertheless three Anglican Priests and members of the A.P.U.C., F.G. Lee, T.W. Mossman and J.R. Seccombe managed to get themselves consecrated Bishops of the English Uniate Church in northern Italy during the Summer of 1877, and at the subsequent Synod they formed 'The Order of the Corporate Reunion' (O.C.R.). Hardly surprisingly the effects of the Uniate scheme within Anglicanism were neglible.

De Lisle and other members of the A.P.U.C. were undoubtedly fifty years ahead of their time in attempting to foster ecumenism, as the prerequisite for any ecumenical activity is the belief that the other person's tradition, be it Roman Catholic, Anglican or Orthodox, is a valid expression of the Christian Faith. What the Catholic members of the A.P.U.C. did not realise was that the Roman Church had set its face resolutely against such views and was preparing to demonstrate this by the publication of the Syllabus of Errors and the formulation of the doctrine of Papal Infallability. To the authorities in Rome, who saw only a rising tide of secularism, liberalism and socialism in Europe, what was needed was an explicit declaration of the Catholic position which would have to be authorative and binding on all who called themselves Catholic. That the situation was not seen to be so desperate from Grace Dieu as it did from the Vatican is probably why the Papal

Rescript came as such a shock to De Lisle, but it does suggest that De Lisle's passion for ecumenism rather blinded him to the realities of the situation. He should have realised that a Church headed by Pius IX, led in England by Wiseman, Manning and with a largely Ultramontane Hierarchy, would not take kindly to any suggestion that the Catholic Church should be seen, either explicitly or implicitly, to renounce its claim to possessing a monopoly of truth. The idea of an Anglican Uniate Church was an interesting one, but not a realistic proposition to all but a tiny minority in the Church of England. But it was the only possibility left to the Catholic reunionists after Pius had made it clear that the Vatican's definition of Christian unity was unconditional surrender on the part of 'heretics' before the See of Rome.

Notes

Chapter One

1. See Leetham, C.R. *Ratcliffe College 1847-1947.* The Ratcliffian Association, 1950.
2. See Elliott, B., 'Mount St Bernard's Reformatory or Agricultural College'. Article in *The Adaption of Change: Essays upon the history of nineteenth century Leicester and Leicestershire.*
3. Kimberlin, A.H. *The Return of Catholicism to Leicester: 1746-1946,* Samuel Walker, Hinckley, 1948.

Chapter Two

1. Until the restoration of the hierarchy in 1850 the Catholic Church in England was a Mission Church. Thus Vicars-Apostolic were appointed to Districts rather than Bishops to Dioceses, although all the Vicars-Apostolic were consecrated Bishops. The difference between a Diocesan Bishop and a Vicar-Apostolic was essentially one of title rather than function.
2. Extract: Shrewsbury to De Lisle. September 1836. Gwynn 1947. p28.
3. Extract: Palmer to Madame de Chabannes. 7.11.1836. M.S.B. Archives. Original at Stapehill, Dorset.
4. Extract: De Lisle to Walsh, 22.4.1836. M.S.B. Archives, original in Birmingham Archives.
5. Extract: Founders Deed, 29.9.1839. M.S.B. Archive.
6. Railton's Monastery was used between 1851 and 1881 to house the Reformatory. Today, no trace of it remains.
7. Until Vatican II most Roman Catholic Religious Orders were divided into Choir Monks and Lay Brothers. The Choir Monks spent more time in Choir singing the Office, whilst the Lay Brothers did more work in the monastery and on the farm. This system was open to abuse, as the Lay Brothers could become servants to the Choir Monks and the distinction was abolished by Vatican II.
8. Quoted from Anson, P.F., 1978. p18.
9. See *Garendon Abbey,* by Wallace Humphrey. East Midlands Study Unit, Loughborough University, 1982.

Chapter Three

1. Extract: Manning to Ryder, Whitmonday 1850. M.S.B. Archives
2. Extract: Newman to Woodgate. 19.4.1842. M.S.B. Archives
3. Extract: Newman to Know. 13.1.1846. Letters and Diaries...Vol XI. p93
4. Extract: Newman to Stanton. 27.7.1848. Letters and Diaries...Vol XII. p251.
5. Letter: Palmer to *Leicester Chronicle,* 10.4.1842. M.S.B. Archives
6. From 'A Brief Sketch...' Dolman 1855. p2. M.S.B. Archives
7. From an account of a visit to Mount St Bernard on 24.4.1848. Published in *De La Renaissance Catholique en Angleterre,* Paris, 1849.
8. Extract: Palmer to Lady Shrewsbury, 22.4.1846. M.S.B. Archives
9. Extract: Palmer to *The Tablet,* 15.3.1851. M.S.B. Archives.
10. From *The Tablet,* 20.11.1852
11. From 'A Brief Sketch...' Dolman, 1855. p13. M.S.B. Archives

Chapter Four

1. See Appendix II. Article xxxvii of the Thirty-Nine Articles of Religion.
2. Extract: 'Popery a New Religion...' 1835, p8. M.S.B. Archives.

3. From Odilo Woolfrey's account of the Anne Fullard case. 1835, p5. M.S.B. Archives.
4. Extract: *Special Pleadings...* 1836, p 26. M.S.B. Archives.
5. *ibid.* p27.
6. Extract: De Lisle to Walsh, 22.4.1836. M.S.B. Archives. Original in Birmingham Archives.
7. Extract: 'A Pastoral Address...' 1845, p3. M.S.B. Archives.
8. *ibid.* p4
9. See Fosbroke's *British Monachism* published in 1816 for the classic example of monasticism treated as an historical curiosity with no contemporary relevance.
10. 'A Pastoral Address' *op. cit.* p5.
11. *ibid.*
12. 10. Geo. IV. Cap 17, Sect. 28-29.
13. 'A Pastoral Address' *op. cit.* p11.
14. *ibid.* p13.
15. *ibid.* p15.
16. See Appendix II.
17. 'A Pastoral Address' *op. cit.* p22.
18. *ibid.* p25.
19. *ibid.* p26.
20. *ibid.* p26-7.
21. Extract: Newman to Giberne, 23.7.1849. 'Letters and Diaries...' Vol XIII, p240.
22. Extract: Newman to Ragg, 2.7.1849. 'Letters and Diaries...' Vol XIII p200.
23. Norman, E.R., *Anti-Catholicism in Victorian England,* Allen and Unwin, 1968. p .
24. Duffy. *History Today.* June 1982. p10.

Chapter Five

1. Extract: Rosmini to De Lisle 18.11.1839. Leetham 1965 p119.
2. Extract: Gentili to Rosmini 2.7.1840. Leetham 1965 p128.
3. For more information on Chartism in the Leicester area see: Cooper, T. *The Life of Thomas Cooper* (1872). In a new edition published by Leicester University Press, 1971, with an Introduction by J. Saville.
4. Extract: Gentili to Pagani 26.8.1842. Leetham 1965 p151.
5. Extract: Gentili to Rosmini 8.1.1841. Leetham 1965 p138.
6. Extract: Gentili to Bolangero 4.1.1841. Leetham 1965 p137.
7. Extract: Gentili to his brother. May 1841. Leetham 1965 p138.
8. Extract: Gentili to his brother. May 1842. Leetham 1965 p138.
9. Gentili to Bianchi 13.8.1835. Leetham 1965 p62.
10. Extract: Gentili to Rosmini 20.6.1835. Leetham 1965 p61.

Chapter Six

1. Leetham 1965 p130.
2. Cooke, 1879 Ch X, pp142-3
3. Extract: Gentili to Taylor 6.7.1840. Leetham 1965 p134.
4. *ibid.*
5. Appendix III.
6. Pagani (elder). Richardson, London 1851.
7. Gwynn 1951 p173-4

Chapter Seven

1. Extract: Gentili to Rosmini 17.9.1842. Leetham 1965 p148.
2. Extract: Gentili to Rosmini June 1843. Leetham 1965 p150.
3. Leetham 1965 p153.
4. Extract: Gentili to Pagani 19.5.1846. Leetham 1965 p155.
5. Duffy. *History Today,* June 1982, p10.
6. *ibid,* p11.
7. *ibid,* p11.
8. Pagani (elder) Richardson, London.

Appendices

1. Anson, P.F. 1978, p14.
2. M.S.B. Archives
3. M.S.B. Archives
4. Purcell, E.S., 1900, Vol I p415.
5. Extract: De Lisle to Editor of *Union* 20.12.1864. Purcell 1900, Vol I, p400.

Bibliography

Primary Sources

Founders Deed 1839: Phillipps (De Lisle) to Mount St Bernard (Cistercian Order). M.S.B. Archives

'"Popery" a New Religion, compared with that of Christ and His Apostles'. Sermon of Rev Francis Merewether 24.5.1835. M.S.B. Archives

'To the Inhabitants of the Parish of Whitwick'. Account by Odilo Woolfrey of the cure of Anne Fullard, December 1835. M.S.B. Archives

'Special Pleadings in the Court of Reason and Conscience...' Rev Francis Merewether 20.3.1836. M.S.B. Archives

'A Pastoral Address to the Inhabitants of Whitwick, Leicestershire, On the opening of a Monastery within the Limits of that Parish.' Rev Francis Merewether, 1845. M.S.B. Archives.

'A Full Report of a Most Extraordinary Investigation which took place on Tuesday, 26th June 1849 at Mount St Bernard Monastery, Leicestershire.' M.S.B. Archives.

Secondary Sources

General

Anson, P.F. *Building Up the Waste Places,* The Faith Press 1978.

Clark, K. *The Gothic Revival: An Essay in the History of Taste,* John Murry, 1962.

Gash, N. *Aristocracy and People — Britain 1815-1865,* Edward Arnold, 1979.

Holmes, J.D. *More Roman than Rome,* Burns and Oates, 1978.

Holmes, J.D. *The Triumph of the Holy See,* Burns and Oates, 1978

Mitchell, D., *The Jesuits, A History,* Macdonald, 1980.

Vidler, A.R., *The Church in an Age of Revolution,* Penguin, 1980.

Specific

'A Brief Sketch of the Life of the Rt Rev John Bernard Palmer: First Lord Abbot of the Cistercian Abbey of Mount St Bernard, Leicestershire, and the first mitred Abbot in England since the Reformation'. Published by C. Dolman, London, 1855.

Berkeley, J., *Lulworth and the Welds,* The Blackmore Press, 1971.

Bossy, J., *The English Catholic Community 1570-1850,* London 1975.

Cooke, Fr R. (O.M.) *Sketches of the Life of Mgr de Mazenod and Oblate Missionary Labours,* 2 volumes, London 1879.

Dessain, C.S. (ed.) *The Letters and Diaries of John Henry Newman,* Vols XI, XII, XIII, Nelson and Sons Ltd.

Gwynn, D, *Father Luigi Gentili and his Mission. 1801-1848,* Clonmore and Reynold Press 1951.

Gwynn, D, *The Return of Catholicism to Leicester: 1746-1946,* Samuel Walker, Hinckley, 1948.

Lacey, A.J. and Smith, S., et al, *A History of Shepshed (Regis),* Freeman Press Ltd, Shepshed, 2nd ed 1969.

Leetham, C.R., *Luigi Gentili: A Sower of the Second Spring'* Burns and Oates, 1965

Leetham, C.R., *Ratcliffe College, 1847-1947,* The Ratcliffian Association, 1950.

Norman, E.R., *Anti-Catholicism in Victorian England,* Allen and Unwin, 1968.

Purcell, E.S. *Life and Letters of Ambrose Phillipps de Lisle,* 2 volumes, Macmillan and Co. 1900.

Wilson, A., *Blessed Dominic Barbari, C.P.,* Sands and Co Ltd, 1967.

Pamphlets and Articles

Rosminian Notes Vol II, No VI, March 1961.

St Mary's Loughborough, The Early Years

Bozzetti, Dr J., *Aloysius Gentili of the Fathers of Charity,* Milan 1938

Yates, N., *The Oxford Movement and Anglican Ritualism,* The Historical Association, 1983

Duffy, E. 'The Bishop of Rome and the Catholics of England', *History Today,* June 1982, pp5-12.

Br Jonathan Gell, 'The Return of the Cistercians to England', *Hallel: A Review of Monastic Spirituality and Liturgy,* Summer, 1982.

Robbins, K., 'Papal Progress' *History Today,* June 1982, pp13-17.